W9-BQL-407

We Need Silence to Find Out What We Think

We Need Silence to Find Out What We Think

SELECTED ESSAYS

Shirley Hazzard

Edited with an Introduction
by Brigitta Olubas

Columbia University Press
New York

Boca Raton Public Library

Columbia University Press
Publishers Since 1893
New York Chichester, West Sussex
cup.columbia.edu
Copyright © 2016 Columbia University Press
All rights reserved

Library of Congress Cataloging-in-Publication Data

Hazzard, Shirley, 1931–
[Essays. Selections]
We need silence to find out what we think : selected essays /
Shirley Hazzard ; edited with an introduction by Brigitta Olubas.
pages cm
Includes bibliographical references and index.
ISBN 978-0-231-17326-1 (cloth : acid-free paper) —
ISBN 978-0-231-54079-7 (e-book)
I. Olubas, Brigitta, editor. II. Title.

PR9619.3.H369A6 2016
824'.914—dc23 2015016426

Columbia University Press books are printed
on permanent and durable acid-free paper.
This book is printed on paper with recycled content.
Printed in the United States of America

c 10 9 8 7 6 5 4 3 2 1

Cover design: Catherine Casalino
Cover photo: © Getty/David Levenson

References to websites (URLs) were accurate at the time
of writing. Neither the author nor Columbia University Press
is responsible for URLs that may have expired or changed
since the manuscript was prepared.

CONTENTS

ACKNOWLEDGMENTS

It has been a privilege to edit this selection of Shirley Hazzard's nonfiction writings. I would like first of all to thank the author for permission to reproduce here the unpublished essays and the published work for which she holds copyright, and also for granting me access to her private archives and working manuscripts. This access was facilitated in formal and practical ways by Frances Alston and Annabel Davis-Goff, and I would like to express my gratitude to both. I also wish to thank staff at the Rare Book and Manuscript Library, Columbia University, for their assistance with Hazzard's papers held there. I undertook a large part of the work of editing this material while a visiting scholar at Wolfson College, University of Oxford, in 2014, and I am grateful for the welcome and support provided by colleagues there. My work has also been greatly helped by grants and other forms of institutional support from the School of the Arts and Media and the Faculty of Arts and Social Sciences at the University of New South Wales in 2014 and 2015, and an Australian Research Council Discovery Grant (2011–2013): DP110104174, "Shirley Hazzard: Life, Work and Ethical Engagement." My efforts to track down the more arcane references in Hazzard's essays were greatly assisted by Nicholas Birns, and I would also like to express my gratitude to Jonathan Galassi for his help with Hazzard's numerous references to the work of Leopardi and Montale, and to Edward Mendelson for help with some of her references to Auden. I would like once again to acknowledge with thanks the interest and support for my work on Shirley Hazzard shown by Akeel Bilgrami. The collegial and convivial atmosphere provided by my colleagues in the School of the Arts and Media at UNSW has made for a particularly stimulating working environment, and the ongoing support of Bruce and Zoia makes everything possible—thanks to you all. Finally, I would like to thank Jennifer Crewe, Kathryn Schell, and the editorial team at Columbia University Press for their thoughtful and rigorous attention, all of which has helped me to do justice to the task of bringing Shirley Hazzard's remarkable prose into an accessible form for a new audience. Any errors that remain are, of course, mine.

With the publishers, I would like to thank the following for permission to reproduce copyrighted material: the *New York Times* for "We Need Silence to Find Out What We Think," November 14, 1982, 11, 28–29; "A Mind Like a Blade: Review of Muriel Spark," September 29, 1968, 1; "Review of Jean Rhys: *Quartet*," April 11, 1971, 6; "The New Novel by the New Nobel Prize Winner: Review of Patrick White, *The Eye of the Storm*," January 6, 1974, 1, 12; "The Patron Saint of the UN Is Pontius Pilate," February 23, 1974, 31; "'Gulag' and the Men of Peace," August 25, 1974: 446; the *New Republic* for "Where Governments Go to Church," March 1, 1975, 11–14; "The League of Frightened Men: Why the UN Is so Useless," January 19, 1980, 17–20; "UNHelpful: Waldheim's Latest Debacle," April 12, 1980, 10–13; Farrar, Straus and Giroux for "Translating Proust," in ed. André Aciman, *The Proust Project* (1994), 174–181; Editions Slatkine for "The Tuscan in Each of Us," in *An Antipodean Connection: Australian Writers, Artists and Travellers in Tuscany*, ed. Gaetano Huber and Marie Christine Huber (1993), 77–82; James Kirkup/*New Yorker* for "On a Tanaka by Ochi-Ai Naobumi," October 3, 1959, 46. Extracts from W. H. Auden's "The Shield of Achilles," (Copyright © [1955] renewed 1976 and "Letter to Lord Byron" [1937] renewed 1976), are both reprinted by permission of Curtis Brown, Ltd.

INTRODUCTION

SHIRLEY HAZZARD

Author, Amateur, Citizen

BRIGITTA OLUBAS

Shirley Hazzard stands as a distinctive, even idiosyncratic figure in the New York literary scene she inhabited from the middle of the twentieth century. Her significance as a literary author is by now well established; a claim—such as that made implicitly by the publication of this collection—that she might also be viewed, and valued, as a public intellectual rests on the basis of her distinctive life and associations as well as her fiction. She left her native Australia in 1947 as a very young woman, without having completed a formal education, and wound up in New York, where she worked in a relatively lowly capacity for the United Nations from the early 1950s.[1] After resigning her post there to write full time, at first mainly short fiction for the *New Yorker*, she published a number of acclaimed novels. In the early 1960s she met and married the Flaubert scholar Francis Steegmuller, and the couple lived part of each year in Naples and Capri, and part in Manhattan, where their extensive circles of friends and associates included many of the significant literary figures of the time, including those known as the New York Intellectuals.[2]

Hazzard's background and character—an expatriate with no strong ties to her country of origin; an exquisite stylist, skilled linguist, and fiercely intellectual autodidact, deeply immersed in the Western literary canon and committed to the individual apprehension of art; a meticulously informed observer of local and international politics, intent on holding its representatives and practitioners to the highest ideals—

defined in important ways the kind of writer and thinker she became. In many senses, the description by David Daiches of Lionel Trilling, whom Hazzard and Steegmuller knew well, might also apply to her: "in many respects my idea of the perfect New York intellectual . . . intelligent, curious, humane, well read, interested in ideas, fascinated by other places, immensely knowledgeable about European culture."[3] Similarly, Terry A. Cooney's claim that "Western culture as a whole provided the general frame of reference for the *Partisan Review* circle and the widest standard of aspiration; their perspective was consciously and emphatically international," applies readily to Hazzard.[4] With a private income from Steegmuller's first marriage, the couple were able to devote their lives to writing, and to reading. Described in retrospect as "a conjugal version of literary high life," they practiced amateurism or belles lettres at the most elevated levels; producing, on Steegmuller's part, erudite and scholarly biographies of a range of mainly French literary and cultural notables, and translations, principally of Flaubert, and on Hazzard's delicately wrought, thoughtful, morally charged fictions about the newly forming global, or cosmopolitan, postwar world.[5] And also, if to more muted acclaim and less sustained recognition, a succession of nonfiction writings.

This collection brings together for the first time that nonfiction, produced and mostly published in the last three decades of the twentieth century. These essays, lectures, and reviews track Hazzard's acclaimed fiction, echoing, extending, and illumining it; however, the writing of these nonfiction pieces created something of a distraction for their author, drawing her away from her primary labor. Hazzard noted this herself in an interview around her second monograph about the United Nations, *Countenance of Truth* (1990), observing that working on "antipathetic matters of this kind" had taken her away from the "work that I love as a poet" but that she felt that she had had no choice, given the gravity of its subject matter and her sense of her responsibilities as citizen.[6] This sense of her writerly practice as defined in the tensions and contrary demands of the political and the aesthetic, the public and the private domains, is at once instructive and deceptively straightforward as a way of thinking about her work and significance, as I hope this collection of essays will demonstrate. This tension is one of the important features aligning her work with that of the New York Intellectuals, who were editing and publishing in the same journals as Hazzard, and many of whom, as already noted, were her friends. The close fit between art and politics, formed around the figure of the intellectual, is common to most commentaries on this group, with Alexander Bloom arguing that they "held out for the pre-eminence of art, not devoid of social context but reflective of it . . . [and] they held strongly to ideas about the special and crucial role for critics and for intellectuals in general," and Nicholas Birns noting their commitment to "the relationship of literature, especially the novel, to society. They sought to establish a public arena of conversation about literature that would touch on politics and social questions but not be contaminated by or held hostage to them."[7]

Shirley Hazzard has clearly always seen the work of literature, and thus of the literary author, in terms that embrace the domains of politics and art; for her they are not easily or usefully separated. Her fiction—in particular her two larger, later novels *The Transit of Venus* and *The Great Fire* as well as her early collection of satirical stories *People in Glass Houses*—have their action firmly grounded in the world of midcentury public and political life, and also in the interior worlds, sensibilities, and sympathies of their protagonists. Although the primary matter, densely poetic, of her fiction is that of sexual and romantic love, she also deals directly with the recollections and consequences of world war, the administration of peace with all its brutal militarism, ongoing agitations around the world in relation to dissidents and refugees, the pernicious endurance and ineptitude of bureaucracies as well as the expressly political dimensions of the domestic and international policies of diverse governments. These worlds meet most pointedly in the moral and ethical choices presented to protagonists in their personal and professional lives as artists, scientists, activists, lovers, or friends; they are choices that embody a necessary continuity of interior lives and social and political realities. This shared space of art and politics is likewise at the heart of Hazzard's nonfiction.

The essays in this collection were first published in a range of newspapers and magazines, mostly in New York; three of them have never been published before. While some essays about the United Nations appeared in journals associated with the New York Intellectuals, such as the *New Republic* and the *Partisan Review*, there is no sense of a singular or identifiable audience with shared views; rather the impression they give is of a spectrum of perspectives and of a willingness on the author's part to step outside readily identifiable political categories. And this distinctiveness of her political position has led to some unexpected responses to Hazzard's work: for instance, in Mark Mazower's discussion she is characterized as a "conservative" critic of the UN, alongside William F. Buckley Jr., even though her political orientation was consistently of the Left.[8] More broadly, while it is useful to think about Hazzard in the context of the New York Intellectuals, it is also important to bear in mind that she understood herself to be working around and outside such groupings, unaligned in all important matters. Andreea Deciu Ritivoi's recent work on exiled or expatriated "foreign" intellectuals is perhaps useful here, despite the cultural closeness of the United States to Hazzard's country of origin, Australia. Ritivoi observes that the very position of intellectual severs bonds of national affiliation: "intellectuals have always been part of a transnational rather than national order, even before terms like transnationalism and cosmopolitanism became fashionable," adding that "Richard Pell views modern intellectuals as, by the very nature of their mission, outsiders or marginal in relation to any form of power—whether represented by the state, the market, or the university—so as to be able to reflect critically on it."[9]

The essays have been divided into five unequal groupings; this unevenness of volume itself speaks to Hazzard's priorities and also reflects something of the way these writings speak to her biography—the span of her writing life and her priorities in organizing her energies and attention. Part 1 draws its title, "Through Literature Itself," from the first of three lectures Shirley Hazzard presented in early 1982 in the Gauss Seminar series at Princeton University, which are published here for the first time from Hazzard's typescripts. They are preceded by "We Need Silence to Find Out What We Think," published in the *New York Times* later that year, which outlines and defends the importance and the larger demands of literature, its necessity, and the conditions needed for its survival. It is clearly drawn in part at least from the Gauss seminars but is sufficiently distinct to warrant the inclusion of both. The essays in this section give the clearest and most compelling sense of Hazzard's thinking about the place of literature in the contemporary world; they require nonetheless only a brief introduction, as their significance is everywhere evident in their superb prose and the breadth and depth of their reference.

The Lonely Word is Hazzard's title for the three Gauss seminars. In them she takes up with self-conscious gravity the opportunity to speak across the professional/amateur divide as a literary writer and reader, an intellectual from outside the university, providing a very personal but erudite survey of the condition of Western literature in late modernity as trace and exemplar of humanism. Her themes are as follows: in the first lecture "Virgil and Montale," the public role of the poet from the classical to the modern era through the collapse of heroism that attended the rise of Christian thought and aesthetics in the West; in the second, "The Defense of Candor," the relation of poetic language to truth across this same period; and finally in "Posterity: The Bright Reversion," the nature of literary fame and longevity, of poetic remembrance, and of canonicity.

The temporal arc of Western humanistic culture is her initial point of departure. She notes the concurrence of celebrations in Italy the previous year to mark "the two thousandth anniversary of the death of Virgil; and . . . the death [last year], at the age of eighty-four, of Eugenio

Montale," two poets whose work resonates through the three essays. This time frame—she notes that Tennyson's commemoration of Virgil, which provides the title for the series, was composed "just a century ago"—suggests the closeness of bonds between writers as well as the immensity that must be bridged in reading and scholarship, and it offers the occasion for the announcement of her own ethical proof, her right to speak as author, through the practices of literary emulation and apprenticeship. It also grounds the imagined future of poetic posterity; art is "the only afterlife of which we have evidence—the transmission of human experience and thought." Against this expansive background she traces the "diminution of high heroic passion" in modern life and literature as a form of loss, with Auden's "disappearance of the Public Realm as the sphere of revelatory personal deeds" at its heart.

The value of literature thus lies first in its capacity to compensate for or repair loss—"Through art we can feel, as well as know, what we have lost; in art, as in dreams, we can occasionally retrieve and re-experience it"—through its capacity for immediacy, its ability "to transmit sensations and sentiments." That "directness to life" draws from a commitment to the rightful labor of writing and to its veracity, a "responsibility to the accurate word." The only authentic response to literature is through pleasure, and reading is "in part an act of submission, akin to generosity or love; and confession to it, through praise, is a commitment to a private 'unauthorized' response." Hazzard is here presenting a kind of apologia for amateur reading, which speaks to her own role and practice working outside the circuits of professional literary criticism. She is particularly critical of the forms of literary criticism that developed in universities in the second half of the twentieth century.[10] Her amateurism is central to her constitution as an intellectual; it draws on a tradition of literary devotion and is nourished by a privately gleaned intellectual rigor.

Part 2, "The Expressive Word" includes Hazzard's writings on specific works and authors, and focuses more tightly on the practice of literary reading. Its title is taken from her reflection on the particularity of one of her literary friendships, with author Graham Greene: "We were . . . writers and readers in a world where the expressive word, spoken or written, still seemed paramount."[11] These five reviews, from 1968 to 1978, of fiction by the English authors Muriel Spark, Jean Rhys, and Barbara Pym, and by the nineteenth-century Neapolitan Matilde Serao, and the Australian Patrick White, are brought together with four essays published more than a decade later, from 1990 to 2004: a discussion of different translations of Proust; introductions to new editions of two very different, favored works of Hazzard's—Geoffrey Scott's *The Portrait of Zélide* and Iris Origo's biography of Giacomo Leopardi; and an essay memorializing her former *New Yorker* editor and great friend, William Maxwell.

The diversity of these subjects is indicative of the range of Hazzard's literary interests, and the variety and depth of her reading. It constitutes an archive of her personal taste but also suggests a loose map of literary friendships and associations, preferences, and points of familiarity. We might note the career interruptions, the vagaries of late or re-publication in her discussion of Rhys, Pym, and Spark; viewed together these names implicitly suggest the particular attenuation and belatedness that might be seen to characterize the careers of writing women of the mid-twentieth century, including Hazzard's own. Her selection also highlights writers whose subject matter sits just outside identifiable national literary frames; in Rhys, the lives of whose characters flicker around the edges of the "perfectly dreadful little corner of a foreign field" that is Paris, or conversely, Spark and Pym, who exemplify the acerbic complexities and delights of national representativeness. If other writers appear to exemplify local traditions, it is through the lens of the "parochial" or quiescent international ignorance of their worth as with Australia's Nobel laureate Patrick White, or the continuing and tragic aptness a century later of Matilde Serao's writing of conditions that resulted in an outbreak of cholera in Naples.

Hazzard approaches Proust through the prism of translation and great writing, quoting François Guizot on his experience of rereading

Edward Gibbon, whom he had initially dismissed only to find on a "second attentive and regular perusal of the entire work" that he had "exaggerated" the importance of the errors found and was struck now rather by "the immensity of his researches, the variety of his knowledge." This respect for the labor of erudition subtends Hazzard's defense of devoted amateur scholarship, which receives its most expansive and eloquent consideration in her introduction to Iris Origo's biography of Giacomo Leopardi, the poet whose work touches her own perhaps most deeply. Her tribute to William Maxwell provides some sense of the importance of her connections to the *New Yorker* magazine, a rich account of writerly sympathy and, related to both these, a further testament to the belles-lettristic tradition: "Maxwell was not drawn to intellectualism. His gift lay in acute humane perception." The invocation of Francis Steegmuller in her introduction to Geoffrey Scott's *The Portrait of Zélide* is similarly resonant, and she notes as a theme of Scott's book and of Steegmuller's oeuvre a figure, which is also hauntingly suggestive of her own: "the intelligent and gifted woman seeking to ripen and express her best powers; yet carrying within her an ideal of love unlikely to be realised."

The title of Part 3, "Public Themes," is a phrase Hazzard has used to describe her interests and concerns beyond literature. It includes a very small part of the volume of writing she produced on the subject of the United Nations, much of which was brought together in her two monographs on the topic from 1973 and 1990. I have chosen essays that respond to specific events and that voice concerns around which Hazzard was particularly exercised: the compromising of human rights by endemic failings of the UN at an organizational level; the UN's politicized suppression of dissident Soviet author Aleksandr Solzhenitsyn; its failure to protect rights of individual employees from the lower levels of the Secretariat; the moral and personal deficiencies of Secretary-General Kurt Waldheim; and, more subtly, her attention to the ways that global and planetary perspectives might be seen to be forming in the postwar landscape. If Hazzard's output on the subject of the UN and its failings is extensive, that published work sits on an even more massive body of unpublished writings, including hundreds of letters by Hazzard and to her from agents in the matters she is pursuing, or from other commentators, along with press clippings about the UN—many annotated—and internal UN documents, stretching back to the period of her first employment in the early 1950s. This archive speaks voluminously to Hazzard's expressed frustration at being taken away from her work as a writer of fiction as well as to the gravity with which she saw herself a public figure with a profile that could be used to pursue matters of great public weight, and therefore with the responsibility to take on this labor.

It is important to note that much of that work has gone unacknowledged. While Kurt Waldheim's wartime involvement in the Austrian Nazi party became public knowledge during his campaign for the Austrian presidency in 1986, it was Shirley Hazzard who first broke this story in 1980, sparking a preliminary inquiry by US Congressman Stephen Solarz and mendacious denials from Waldheim.[12] Similarly, Hazzard's earlier exposure and analysis in *Defeat of an Ideal* of the extent and impact of FBI investigation of the political orientation of US employees at the UN from its earliest years was one of the first such accounts to be published; her role in documenting these matters is, however, not generally acknowledged.[13] (It has become lost, perhaps, in the sheer volume of her criticisms of the institution.) A third story is worth highlighting here: her investigation and disclosure of the UN's removal of works by the Soviet dissident and Nobel laureate Aleksandr Solzhenitsyn from bookshops on its property in Geneva in 1974. Her approaches generated involvement from PEN American Center, among others, and led to the reinstatement of the works amid assertions from Waldheim and his spokesmen that they had not been removed at all. Hazzard's striking response to these claims, which can be read here in her published letter to the *New York Times*, give some sense of the tone of much of her archived correspondence and illustrates once more the gravity with which she approached her public responsibilities as citizen.

The question of the role and function of the UN continues to perplex and engage writers and the general public today; Tony Judt notes in an essay originally published in 2007, "Is the UN Doomed?" that "the United Nations is a curiously contested topic."[14] And Hazzard's writings on issues such as human rights remain current, indeed urgent, three decades after they were published, as does her consideration of the responsibility of nongovernment bodies to take on issues like human rights that had been so poorly managed by the UN.[15] Her close friendship with Ivan Morris, one of the founders of Amnesty International in the United States, is reflected in her careful tracing of the developing role of this and other NGOs as a counter to the lumbering inaction of the centrally funded world body: "Into the vacuum created by United Nations inaction on human rights has come an active humanitarianism by individuals and private agencies that has gradually formed itself into a moral force—a force of the kind that a different United Nations might have inspired and led."

Hazzard also tracks the UN's efforts to "thwart" and "short-circuit" the expression of public will and concern through these movements as a threat to its own role. Against the hopeful rise of citizens' movements she charts the rising power of multinational corporations—and the rise of their influence within the UN—and she voices concern at the dominance of bureaucratic approaches and of corporate and commerce models in the administration of the UN's agendas, arguing that the UN's "high potential . . . was quickly broken on a wheel of seminars, social events, academicism and Establishment contacts totally removed from perspective and actualities."

The heart of her concern with the United Nations is its inability to represent with any integrity the international scope of the postwar world, partly through the shambling inefficiency of its bureaucratic organization but more through having been compromised by its structural allegiance to what she calls its "archaic pattern of nationalism." In place of the nationalistic investments she finds in the capitulation to both US interests in the McCarthyist surveillance of its UN employees and the Soviet government's pressures around the discrediting and suppression around Solzhenitsyn, she posits a "planetary" allegiance, grounded in the beliefs and actions of citizens, with the hope of generating what she calls, resonantly, "human systems as global as our emergencies." While the kind of critique she makes of the UN might be seen as a feature of her historical location—that is to say, contained within the framing of public debates through the postwar decades around positions identified as "idealist" and "realist"—it is in the end not simply reducible to its context.[16] After all, her claims are meticulously based on factual evidence not mere polemic, as these essays show; she was right all along on Waldheim, on Solzhenitsyn, on Iran, and so on. Further, reading these essays in light of her writings about the public role of literature illuminates the larger sense of public responsibility being enacted in and through them, extending their reach beyond their particular political and world-historical reference, without dulling their pertinence as historical artifacts. Indeed, it is enlightening not only to read them outside of their specific historical context and as themselves now historical documents but also to be able to attend to the larger insights into the global condition of late modernity, the "irresistibly planetary nature of the age" that they provide.

This section closes with an essay that provides a further context for Hazzard's UN writings: "A Writer's Reflection on the Nuclear Age," published in 1982. Preoccupation with the consequences of the deployment and continuing development of nuclear weaponry was of course widespread in the postwar decades, but it is important to note that this concern bore directly on wider perceptions of international cooperation and the role of the United Nations, perceptions that no doubt influence Hazzard through this period.[17] Her essay steps back from a political assessment of the moment of the Hiroshima bombing and its ramifications, although she is keenly aware of the historical urgencies encompassed by the events described. What she provides in place of political analysis is a combination of the direct and domestic experience of youth—"I was dressing to go to school when the announcement came on the radio"—and mature reflection, with the public perspectives it occasions—"the fallout of the bomb on our modern thought and life has been continuous and incalculable." The essay provides a primary if fleeting source for the event itself—"Twenty months after the bomb was dropped I was at Hiroshima"—and for the moral and ethical dilemmas it continued to pose.

The two final sections, "The Great Occasion" and "Last Words" are very much shorter, the first comprising a selection of travel and autobiographical pieces and the second two speeches. "The Great Occasion" draws its title from one of Hazzard's luminous travel essays, "Pilgrimage" (not included here), where she describes witnessing "at the port of Capri a trio of handsome matriarchs . . . gold and silver lace over their coiled hair and on their dresses of *rosso antico* that swept the ground. By their festive costume they honored the great occasion of travel."[18] The individual experience of travel in its contemporary, cosmopolitan, fortunate forms is always bound in Hazzard's writing to its at times unexpected antecedents, to the occasion it provides for confronting the unfamiliar and unknown. Travel works as a kind of touchstone for the rich historical and individual foundation of modernity, a synecdoche for the globalized world that had taken on clear contours by the end of the twentieth century, and which is in itself part of the core matter of Hazzard's novels and stories. It is for this reason that her travel writings constitute in themselves a significant part of the corpus of her work. This section opens with a long essay, just on the brink of narrative, of Hazzard's experiences as a sixteen-year-old living and working in Hong Kong in the immediate aftermath of the Second World War. It is difficult to separate the errors and confusions of youth from those of the foreigner and indeed those of the reflective narrator, looking back after twenty years to a city she knows must now be unrecognizable to her. The protagonist encounters at every turn the constraints and opportunities of life beyond a family unit she cannot wait to shed, alongside tangible signs of her own colonial privilege—"Through some standard injustice, I was led to the front of this crowd"—and, always, the play of weight and inconsequence, familiarity and misrecognition in the apprehension of particular locations both new and remembered.

"Canton More Far" thus forms a graphic counterpoint to "A Writer's Reflections on the Nuclear Age," situating Hazzard's writing self at the middle of the century and in Asia, beyond the more keenly known worlds of Europe, the United States, and Australia, and providing an absorbing foreshadowing of *The Great Fire*. The final two essays in this section add to the corpus of her writings on Italy; both express her delight in and familiarity with their specific locations—Tuscany and Naples—through the actions, cares, and energies of people living or visiting there.

The collection closes with transcripts of Hazzard's last public words, both delivered extempore: the first on the occasion of the National Book Award for *The Great Fire* in 2003, an impromptu response to a speech by Steven King in which he criticized the attention paid to high literature by institutions such as the National Book Awards; and the second her unscripted, unprogramed contribution to a panel discussion about her work and significance "Shirley Hazzard: Literary Icon," hosted by the New York Society Library in 2012. Her voice and tone in both carry the same gravity and thoughtfulness heard in her written pieces, despite their somewhat less formal diction and phrasing. Together they provide succinct recapitulation of the views and perspectives that she has so painstakingly presented over the last half century. There is hopefulness and pleasure—"We have this huge language so diverse around this earth"—along with fear for the future—"I feel very much . . . that the world has a kind of Vesuvius element now." They provide a compelling record of Shirley Hazzard's eloquence, her thoughtfulness, civility, and public generosity, and stand as the final statement of her remarkable career.

We Need Silence to Find Out What We Think

PART 1

Through Literature Itself

WE NEED SILENCE TO FIND OUT WHAT WE THINK

Everyone who writes is asked at some stage, Why? Some writers give replies to that question, but I wonder if it is truly answerable. If there is a worthy response, it would to my mind have to do with a wish to close the discrepancy between human experience, with all its strangeness of the mind, as it is known to each of us, and as it is generally expressed. We live in a time when past concepts of an order larger than the self are dwindling away or have disappeared—the deference of the human species and of societies to nationhood, to social systems. The testimony of the accurate word is perhaps the last great mystery to which we can make ourselves accessible, to which we can still subscribe.

Horace wrote that strong men had lived before Agamemnon, but they lacked a poet to commemorate them, and thus passed into oblivion.[1] A modern Italian poet, Eugenio Montale, reminds us, however, that memory existed as a literary genre before writing was invented: men who lived before Agamemnon were not in their time unreported or unsung.[2] Articulation is central to human survival and self-determination, not only in its commemorative and descriptive functions but in relieving the soul of incoherence. Insofar as expression has been matched to sensation and perception, human nature has seemed to retain consciousness. A sense of deliverance plays its part in the pleasure we feel in all the arts and perhaps most of all in literature.

I say most of all in literature because language, unlike other arts, is a medium through which we all deal continually in daily life.

William Butler Yeats said that "if we understand our own minds, and the things that are striving to utter themselves through our minds, we move others, not because we have thought about those others, but because all life has the same root."[3] In its preoccupation with the root of life, language has special responsibilities. Its manipulation, and deviation from true meaning, can be more meaningful than in the case of other arts. And there are always new variations on old impostures, adapted to the special receptivity of the times. In our era, even the multiple possibilities for valid approaches to truth through language are themselves circuitous and increasingly insistent on their successive claims to be "definitive." In repudiating such pretensions from the Realists and other self-styled "schools," Flaubert says, "There is no 'true.' There are merely different ways of perceiving truth."[4]

Through art, as in dreams, we can experience this truth, this root of life, as Yeats calls it. Through art, we can respond ideally to truth as we cannot in life. To suggest the nature of that truth—which is the writer's "material"—I should like to go outside literature for a moment and draw on the view of a painter—Veronese, who in 1572 was called before the Holy Office at Venice to explain why, in a painting of the Last Supper, he had included figures of loiterers, passers-by, people scratching themselves, deformed people, a man having a nosebleed, and so on: details then held unfit to appear in a holy subject. When this grave charge of blasphemy was pressed on Veronese by the examiners, who asked him why he had shown such profane matters in a holy picture, he replied, "I thought these things might happen."[5]

Despite the convoluted theories expended on the novelist's material, its essence is in those words. Paraphrasing a text from Revelation 15:3, W. H. Auden wrote in his poem "The Novelist," that the novelist must "among the Just / Be just, among the Filthy, filthy too, / And in his own weak person, if he can, / Must suffer dull all the wrongs of Man."[6]

The task of the poet or novelist is to convey states of mind and of being as immediately as possible, through language. Immediacy of language is not always or necessarily simplicity, although simplicity is a highly desirable and immensely difficult literary instrument. Valéry says that of two words, we should always choose the lesser.[7] But we don't always have a lesser word that meets out need—although it can be said that veracity tends to express itself with an eminent simplicity, in art as in life; just as discursiveness can often be an index of falsehood.

Without diminishing the merits and advantages of brevity, however, literature cannot be looked on as a competition to employ as few words as possible. Rather it is a matter of seeking accurate words to convey a human condition. And of deploying words so that tone, context, sound, and syntax are ideally combined, without a show of contrivance. That is the proper and agonizing business of literature, in which much of the writer's suffering originates: "the intolerable wrestle with words and meanings," as T. S. Eliot called it.[8] Every writer who is serious about his craft experiences a sense of profaning pure meaning with unworthy words.

Flaubert told George Sand: "When I come on a bad assonance or a repetition in my sentences, I'm sure I'm floundering in the false. By searching I find the proper expression, which was always the only one, and which is also harmonious. The word is never lacking when one possesses the idea. Is there not, in this precise fitting of parts, something eternal, like a principle? If not, why should there be a relation between the right word and the musical word? Or why should the greatest compression of thought always result in a line of poetry?"[9]

Great practitioners of language have supplied new words and new usages when, in the literal sense, words failed them. In most cases, we echo their innovations unthinkingly, because they satisfy, they meet the case. At other times, they bear the maker's seal so distinctly that they can't be uttered without a mental nod in the author's direction. But these great innovators cannot provide a pattern for lesser talents; as Jacques Barzun has said, magnitude creates its own space.[10] More usually, the writer works with words in common use, developing as great a range and as original and independent a voice as possible.

Some writers will bring the whole weight of considered language to their task. Some build their impression in single strokes—whether light or powerful. For the imaginative writer, words must be the measure of talent—to an extent not necessarily true for writers dealing in information and "ideas." The intentions of a novelist or poet are, of course, important, but he or she must be judged on gifts of expression that may not be commensurate with them. The intentions of a historian or a critic, on the other hand, form the basis of our ultimate judgment of his writings, whatever his abilities or deficiencies of communication. The ear of the imaginative writer is ideally tuned to the highest sensitivity, and his distinctive method of transcription is perhaps somewhat misleadingly called style. It is, I think, a recurring error of criticism to treat "style" as an insubstantial literary contrivance distinct from the author's so-called material. Asked to justify his employment of "fine allusions, bright images, and elegant phrases," Dr. Johnson replied with what might be an ideal definition of style: "Why sir, all these ornaments are useful, because they obtain an easier reception for the truth."[11]

I have said that language bears special responsibilities: The writer's vigilance over language and attention to language are themselves an assumption of responsibility. When, with the Renaissance drama, men and women began to speak—through literature—with individual voices, rather than as types (as they had done in medieval morality plays), there was a humanistic assumption of personal accountability for what was uttered. And so we have continued, in theory at least, to regard it. Our words, whether in literature or in life, are accepted as a revelation of our private nature, and an index of the measure of responsibility we are prepared to assume for it.

Even the most imposing speech can, of course, be a confession of evasion. Evasion is rooted in fear, just as responsibility arises from conviction; and the sense of private responsibility through words has proved very hard to maintain. George Orwell said that in order to write fearlessly, one must think fearlessly; and for this it is necessary to have an independent mind.[12] We see that the medieval forms of class and collective responsibility provided a shelter that has been sought ever since through linguistic distortion and pretension.

Our modern age is peculiarly afflicted in this way. Along with the transforming powers of technology and mass society, there developed in the nineteenth century a sort of Industrial Revolution in human expression—an increasing tendency to renounce personal opinion in favor of generalized or official opinion, and to evade self-knowledge and self-commitment through use of abstractions: a wish, in fact, to believe in some process of feeling more efficient than the human soul. There was also an associated new phenomenon of mass communications and mass advertising—that, of new words and usages not spontaneously but speciously brought into wide circulation as a means of profitably directing the human impulse. (The word "jargon," incidentally, anciently derives from the twittering of geese.)

This measure of renunciation of independent and eccentric views that accompanied the growth of mass culture has inevitably infected aesthetic matters. The public has been encouraged, in some quarters, to put its faith in a self-appointed critical authority that, in the words of one modern critic, will "deal expertly" with literature and other arts, relieving readers of time-consuming burdens of private response and private choice. While commentary and scholarly attention have always been directed toward literature and always will be, an entirely new modern industry has grown up of "interpretation." (I make this distinction with the past in the same spirit that a certain schoolmaster in England used to tell his students: "Remember that the intellectual is to the scholar as the cad once was to the gentleman.")

A body of attitudes has developed that seeks to neutralize the very directness to life that is nurtured by art, and to sever the private bond, the immortal intimacy, that has existed between reader and writer. The great writers do not write as if through intermediaries. The new phenomenon is notably one of explication rather than comprehension—the concept of art as a discipline to be contained within consistent laws, the seductive promise of a technology to be mastered by those who will then be equipped to dictate and regiment taste. All this turns on what W. H. Auden called the inability of certain critics to acknowledge that works of art can be more important than anything critics can say about them. As an ominous result we are getting, in literature, an increasing response not to poems and novels but to interpretations. Not to the thing but to the self. While the students of such interpreters can—and do—expound their mentors' views by the hour, it has become very rare to hear them spontaneously quote a line of poetry.

It is always tempting, of course, to impose one's view rather than to undergo the submission required by art—a submission akin to that of generosity or love—that evokes the private response rather than the authorized one. But art is not technology and cannot be "mastered." It is an endless access to revelatory states of mind, a vast extension of living experience and a way of communing with the dead. An intimacy with truth, through which, however much instruction is provided and absorbed, each of us must pass alone.

The degradation of language in the extreme versions of these current explicatory approaches to the arts should be the first concern of anyone wishing to penetrate them. The supposedly "clinical" approach to art necessitates a dehumanized and labored vocabulary and a tone of infectious claims to higher seriousness—a seriousness that proposes itself as superior to art. The unconscious of the modern critical body deserves some exploration, if only to probe its effects on the life of the imagination and to discover why critics of this kind so seldom step aside to allow art to speak, inimitably, for itself—art frequently appearing in their discussions as "mere material" for dissection and classification, and for self-advancement.

Every child knows that it is easier to dismantle a complex creation than to reassemble it. Of similar pedants, Seneca wrote that "No one lets humanity down quite so much as those who study knowledge as if it were a negotiable skill."[13] And it may be that what we suffer from now is simply a new stage of the immemorial attempt to exorcise great mysteries that are inimical to human vanity. I would attach it also to a modern incapacity for wholeness, for synthesis. The power of a work of art ultimately derives not from classifiable components but from an enigmatic quality of synthesis, which does not lend itself to analysis. We do not know why art should exist or why a few human beings should be capable of producing it and even fewer of doing so with enduring excellence. We are often unable even to discern such gifts clearly during an artist's lifetime.

To return from these heights to my own case: I may say that I have found that a great deal of literary discussion seeks to impose consistency for the purpose of proposing "patterns." Of course, some writers work according to a more readily recognizable method than others do. Yet I think that each author's approach—and to each of his own works—will differ. Writers share common difficulties, but they nurture individual ways of contending with them. Similarly, in the work itself, I think that "form" means little unless the quality brought to it can seize it as an opportunity. Like style, form is after all simply the idiosyncratic way one has discovered to convey one's idea.

For me, the ear has an essential role in literary meaning. The arrangement of words, phrases, sentences should sound on the mental ear as effectively as possible, in the silence of the writer's intimacy with his or her reader. For both writer and reader, this is a sensibility refined by reading—that is, through love of literature. For the writer it is often intuitively present in the work—if by intuition we understand a synthesis of intelligence, understanding, and feeling. And it will be intuitively felt and enjoyed by the reader if it is effective. These matters are not devices to pull the wool over the reader's eyes: They are attempts to regain that shared root of life of which Yeats wrote.

The other question most asked of a novelist is to what extent he or she is autobiographically present in the work. Much modern fiction particularly invites that inquiry. Again, any reliable answer will vary greatly from one author to another. And—I should add—there are rather few reliable answers: authors are unlikely to lay all their cards on the table; there is no reason why they should. For myself,

I feel that I drew more on private and even subjective experience when I was first writing and that this diminished as time went on. Even in the first stories I wrote, whole lives and scenes came into my imagination without apparent basis in my acquaintance with life. When we speak of "writing from experience," we usually define experience as whatever has happened directly—or merely—to ourselves. That was to some extent my youthful view. As I got older my experience became more and more what I observed in others, what I imagined of other lives, what I could divine of the infinite range of human possibilities. Thus one may come to speak of writing from experience without simply referring to events and sensations directly affecting oneself.

The author reveals himself, to some degree, in almost any work of fiction, whether intentionally or inadvertently; whether in incidental disclosures or in a gradual emanation of personality. There seems no need for esthetic or "moral" regulation of this—even though it has been a subject of critical "decrees." I enjoy what Byron called the author's "addresses from the throne"[14] if they are done well enough and are seen as part of an inspired whole—as in Dickens or George Eliot or Hardy or Conrad, where author's asides are numerous. Again, it seems to me a question of the order of talent. Anything whatever may be achieved by genius. Or, at the least, the scope and power of genius may make acceptable to us features that are intolerable in lesser talents.

The last theme I would like to touch on is the context in which work is produced. The attempt to touch truth through a work of imagination requires an inner center of privacy and solitude. We all need silence—both external and interior—in order to find out what we truly think. I have come more and more to value the view of Ortega y Gasset that "without a certain margin of tranquility, truth succumbs."[15] However passionate the writer's material, some distance and detachment are needed before the concept can be realized. In our time, the writer can expect little or nothing in the way of silence, privacy, or removal from the deafening clamor of "communications," with all its disturbing and superfluous information. In addition, novelty and the merely up-to-date are urged on writers not only in the name of innovation but virtually as some new form of moral obligation, while critical explication hovers like a vulture. Social continuity and social order—or even the illusion of these—are so disrupted as to have almost gone out of business. The sense of territory and the identity of one's readers are similarly obscured or dispersed. The necessary margin of tranquility for creative work must now presumably be developed somehow in the writer's own consciousness. That involves the exclusion of many other claims—including rightful ones—if one is to preserve some inwardness amid the din.

The poet Montale, whom I mentioned earlier, spoke not long before his recent death of the modern rejection of solitude and singularity, saying that "the wish to huddle in groups, to create noise, and to escape from thought is a sign of desperation and despair." He said that the need to accept a group ideology and generational conformity is contrary to the nature of art and of poetry. Similarly, for the artist, Montale said that the subordination to a method of thinking that one has not worked toward oneself implies a surrender to uniformity, to officialism: "Only the man who lives in solitude can speak of the fatal isolation we all suffer under this inhuman, mass-produced communication. Being in fashion and famous now seems the only accepted role for the contemporary artist. . . . And I ask myself where this absurd absence of judgment will lead us."[16]

This brings me around to my starting point. There is at least one immense truth which we can still adhere to and make central to our lives—responsibility to the accurate word. It is through literature that the word has been preserved and nourished, and it is in literature that we find the candor and refreshment of truth. In the words of Jean Cocteau, the good and rightful tears of the reader are drawn simultaneously by an emotion evoked through literature, and by the experience of seeing a word in place.[17]

THE LONELY WORD

1. VIRGIL AND MONTALE

Last September in Italy, two events were simultaneously honored: at Naples, the two thousandth anniversary of the death of Virgil; and, at Milan, the death, at the age of eighty-four, of Eugenio Montale. The Virgilian ceremonies at Naples were an intensification of bimillennial commemorations, which included public readings of the *Aeneid*, dozens of scholarly articles in daily newspapers (which also carried special weekend color supplements on the poet), and innumerable other observances engaging the entire Neapolitan populace and noted throughout the Italian nation—as, by scholars, throughout the world. In the cathedral of Milan, the funeral of Montale was attended by the president and premier of Italy; while outside the Duomo an immense crowd stood in hot sun, breaking—as a newspaper reported—into "oceanic applause" as the poet's coffin emerged. Banner headlines announcing Montale's death were followed over many days by special newspaper pages of appreciation and reminiscence and, of course, examples of the poet's work. A private memorial, only relatively less public than that held at Milan, subsequently took place at Florence.

It may thus be said that the press of Italy was to a great extent occupied, throughout the month of September 1981, in paying tribute to two poets who died just two thousand years apart, neither of whom had courted popular attention.

At his death in his fifty-first year, Virgil left the twelve books of his *Aeneid*, written in the latter part of his life and apparently completed in 19 BC, the epic that through subsequent centuries has stood in the civilized Western consciousness as a chief literary representation of man's high heroic struggle to transcend his mortality and fulfill, by historic lofty actions, his greater destiny; its theme simply and grandly stated in its celebrated opening words: "Arms and the man I sing."

Montale, in a brief poem written in *his* later life—a poem about a lost cat on a city street—tells us that on that street in past years—that is, during the fascist era—there had occurred events "fit for history, unfit for memory" (*Fatti degni di storia, indegni di memoria*).[1]

So we have two poets, each a master of language and literary form, each accorded in life the highest formal recognition: the one favored by Augustus, the other a Nobel laureate; born in the same peninsula: one near Mantua, the other at Genoa; both profoundly affected by the public events of their troubled times; both of plain, respectable parentage. The public destiny proclaimed by the one as indivisible from the private; by the other, our contemporary, scorned as a contamination with which no decent person can associate himself. In the one, human existence ideally ennobled by superhuman striving. By the other, existence justified only on its most intimate terms.

In considering this mighty reversal during my talk this evening, I make no attempt to unravel the multiplicity of sociological, historical, political, anthropological, and demographic factors contributing to it. Still less do I wish to develop any literary theory, or to seem to pit one poet against another. Art is not a competition. Rather, I should like to offer, as a writer, some comments and conjectures through literature itself. That is, to trace this change through the work of poets and writers themselves, in whom consciousness of it has been acute and continuous. Indeed, the testimony is so vast that it allows tonight only of a few selected indications.

The scene last September in the piazza at Milan may be the last such observance that will occur—the last public tribute to the poet as a recognized requirement of society. (I might add that a young relative of Montale's expressed the view to me at the time that the occasion was exploited by the attending politicians. However that may be, we can't have it every way: at least they acknowledged by their presence that there was something there to exploit.)

I hope not to be misunderstood in speaking of the *function* of the poet. It is not, of course, the business of an artist to give satisfaction as if he were some sort of home appliance, but to enlarge our sensation and perception of life. In contrast to this role of the poet in past societies, W. H. Auden told us that his own passport gave his profession as "writer," because "poet" would have embarrassed people and would have been implausible since, in his words, "everybody knows that nobody now can earn a living by writing poetry." Auden goes on to give four categories of special difficulty for the artistic vocation, and particularly the literary one, in our times:

> Loss of belief in the eternity of the physical universe
> Loss of belief in the significance and reality of sensory phenomena
> Loss of belief in a norm of human nature requiring the same kind of man-fabricated world as its home
> The disappearance of the public realm as the sphere of revelatory personal deeds.[2]

These are all categories of loss—loss for which, in the domain of the arts, nothing fundamental has been substituted. Loss has ever been a constant, in literature, as in life. Every civilized person is familiar with Virgil's beautiful invocation of the tears that underlie human transience—tears that Juvenal considered the noblest of human attributes. But the dimensions, character, and acceleration of loss in the contemporary world have created a *context* of loss amounting to a black hole of the spirit. In the poetry of Montale, loss is a dominant preoccupation—loss of a cat, a shoehorn, a landscape, an attitude, of solitude, of silence. Even his famous simile of the faith that burned like a stubborn log in a fire is of something consuming itself—literally, to ashes. Beyond this, it can be said that at times the poems of Montale approach a veritable celebration of loss.

In a pronouncement central to his thought and work—and also to his times, which are our own fateful era—Montale has told us that every human illusion has found its matching disillusionment: "*Ogni illusione è in perfetta corrispondenza con la sua delusione.*"[3]

It is the fourth of Auden's lost categories that most touches my theme this evening: the disappearance of the public realm as the sphere of revelatory personal deeds. In consequence, Auden says, literature has lost its traditional principal human subject, the man of action, the doer of public deeds. To the ancient world, the private sphere was ruled by mere necessity of sustaining life; whereas the public realm was the field in which a man might disclose and fulfill himself. Today, the public has become the necessary impersonal sphere; while the private leaves us our only hope of manifesting—not even perhaps virtue but merely an individual presence, a singular experience, some affinity with our fellow beings.

The setting for public action is similarly degraded. In Auden's poem, "The Shield of Achilles," Thetis, the mother of Achilles, looks over the shoulder of the armorer Hephaestos to discover—in an invocation of the *Iliad*—what contemporary embellishments he has set on the shield her son will bear to the modern struggle. You'll remember the poem opens:

She looked over his shoulder
For vines and olive-trees,
Marble, well-governed cities
And ships upon untamed seas,
But there on the shining metal
His hands had put instead
An artificial wilderness
And a sky like lead.

A plain without a feature, bare and brown,
No blade of grass, no sign of neighborhood,

Nothing to eat, and nowhere to sit down,
Yet congregated on its blankness stood
An unintelligible multitude.
A million eyes, a million boots in line,
Without expression, waiting for a sign.

And the poem moves on to its doom-laden conclusion:

The thin-lipped armorer
Hephaestos, hobbled away,
Thetis of the shining breasts
Cried out in dismay
At what the god had wrought
To please her son, the strong
Iron-hearted man-slaying Achilles
Who would not live long.[4]

(I might add that Auden also wrote a poem called "Secondary Epic," which begins "No, Virgil, No."and later, "No, Plato, No."[5])

Scepticism about arms and armory is common in the work of poets, including Virgil. To poets, swords have always been double-edged. Rochester says, in his *Satyr against Mankind*: "Whilst wretched man is still in arms for fear. / For fear he arms, and is of arms afraid, / By fear to fear successively betrayed."[6] In the Second World War, Henry Reed literally and figuratively took a gun apart in his delightful "The Naming of Parts."[7]

The overall title of these lectures, "The Lonely Word" is taken from Tennyson's memorial poem on Virgil, where the English laureate finds in the Roman—to quote—"All the charm of the Muses / Often flowering in a lonely word."[8] Tennyson's poem was written just a century ago, at the request of the city of Mantua, for the nineteen hundredth anniversary of Virgil's death; in an era when, as later, in the 1940s, in my own Australian schooldays, every British schoolchild was obliged to study Virgil. In the poem, Tennyson claims to have loved Virgil from his earliest youth—this was also the claim of Berlioz, on rather stronger evidence. I was a child when I first read Tennyson's poem for the first time. Such is the inevitability with which poetry sets its seal on occasions that it did not occur to me then—and scarcely later—that there would be another such anniversary, and that I might be present for it. Still less could I imagine celebrating it, as I did, among the still highly recognizable settings of Book 6 of the *Aeneid*. For me, Tennyson had commemorated Virgil once and for all—Tennyson, whose commemorative powers were demonstrated as early as his fifteenth year when, in 1824, he carved on a rock BYRON IS DEAD.

As I shall revert to this poem of Tennyson's in a later lecture, I shall say a word about it now. The poem touches briefly on the equivocal nature of poetic material—whether mighty or intimate, or the two converging; whether speaking of its time, or for all time, or the two simultaneously; whether it should develop a legend or express a man. Tennyson's famous conclusion is a tribute to this encompassing power of language itself:

> Now the Rome of slaves hath perish'd
> and the Rome of freemen holds her place,
> I, from out the Northern Island
> Sunder'd once from all the human race,
> I salute thee, Mantovano,
> I that loved thee since my day began.
> Wielder of the stateliest measure
> Ever moulded by the lips of man.[9]

The attitudes of which I speak this evening, and their intensifying alteration in recent generations, are being addressed in relation to that power of great language. Many poets—Virgil not least of them—have struggled with the dichotomy of the helpless yet historically conscious human soul ground under by cosmic indifference. In the *Georgics* Virgil praises the good fortune of the farmer living far from battles, attached to realities of earth. Seneca speculates on the possibility of civilizing mankind by teaching the young, as he says, not the crimes of a Philip or Alexander, but the beneficent qualities of existence. The theme is taken up by writers throughout centuries—many of them expressing, as Virgil in the *Eclogues*, ambiguities of feeling in the shadow of history or within the perspective of nature. Virgil tells us that when he set himself to write of kings and battles, Apollo plucked him by the ear—that is, by the source of memory—warning him rather to "woo with slender reed the philosophic muse."[10]

But these divisions of human literary impulse took place, with however many fluctuations and unrealities, within a recognizable context of attitudes to external forces, a *mentalité* acknowledging external forces, a collective necessity greater than the self. Whether achieved or not, some equilibrium was immemorially held necessary to balance human existence in relation to natural and supernatural power: the Greek *Dike*, which saw individualism literally as "idiotic." (In English, by the way, the word "idiot" retained something of that ancient meaning into the seventeenth century.)

In two brief poems called "History," Montale describes the remorseless impersonality of public events, speaking of history's detestation for details, for the "idiotic." He depicts history as a great net with an occasional small tear through which some fish may once in a while slip out: the escaped fish does not even realize he is outside; while those looking on from the net tell themselves they are freer than he.[11]

An accepted starting point for this diminution of high heroic passion is the advent of the Christian era. Literature, however, shows us that human equivocation about single-mindedness was already a common topic. And for expressing these heresies, literature paid an inevitable price and the poet lost ground in his sacred function. In his *Paideia*, Werner Jaeger says that

> the idea that poetry is not useful to life first appears among the ancient theorists of poetics; it was the Christians who finally

> taught men to appraise poetry by a purely aesthetic standard—a standard which enabled them to reject most of the moral and religious teaching of the classical poets as false and ungodly, while accepting the formal elements of their work as instructive and aesthetically delightful.[12]

Even so, St. Jerome expiated his love of pagan texts in the desert, and the Christian convert Paulinus wrote to Ausonius that "Hearts vowed to Christ have no welcome for the goddesses of song; they are barred to Apollo."[13]

The Christian ideal retained the concept of mission. The Golden Bough had been supplanted by the Holy Grail, but with the profound difference that whereas the epic hero became godlike—larger than life—God had assumed Man's daily likeness. Christ is an anti-hero. Man's higher calling was now—at least, ideally—to godliness, meekness, obscurity, simplicity; to pacific and childlike ways; however much ferocity might still take place in the name of salvation. The literary hero remains to some extent familiar—he is necessarily beset on his life's journey by doubt, despair, danger, terror, grief, responsibility, and above all by a temptation to self-indulgence supremely personified as Woman. In letting his choice fall on Aphrodite, Paris had chosen the gratification of private pleasure and disturbed the balance of a larger good. In consequence, his birthplace was destroyed and its survivors turned loose to wander the earth. For succumbing to the inducements of Eve, Adam was banished from Paradise. As Yeats remarked, "What theme had Homer but original sin?"[14] The worst cross the Christian hero has to bear is frequently Woman—Eve, Guinevere, Isolde, Tasso's Armida, Lady Macbeth. Literary Woman is henceforth a debilitating, or, as with Beatrice and Laura, is a redeeming influence on men and so she long remained.

Conversely, by abandoning Dido, and nobly pursuing his higher calling, Aeneas is enabled to found the Italian nation. For this he was commended by St. Augustine, in the City of God, as a pattern for

Christian virtue—St. Augustine remarking with approval that Virgil allowed Dido's tears to fall in vain.[15]

The pattern persisting through the morality plays and the medieval romance, and restated in *The Pilgrim's Progress*, is strongly present in the nineteenth-century novel, and still discernible in modern fiction. It represents perhaps on the part of society an innate yearning toward exemplarity and also toward a caste system that survives in the figure of the knight (who belongs to what is significantly called the nobility). The knight gradually merges in literature with the man of honor, and subsequently with the merely estimable man, while humility contented itself with successive versions of Everyman.

As we see from St. Augustine's comment, the phenomenon of Duty had supplanted the sacrifices required by pagan gods. Yet it was a "Duty" persistently supernatural enough for Wordsworth to address it, fifteen centuries later, as "Stern daughter of the voice of God."[16]

Running parallel or counter to this literary stream, and often mingling with it, was the irrepressible questioning of men by man, a sifting of human conduct refreshed by the Renaissance that showed early traces of the anti-hero. The survival of the pagan gods, to borrow the phrase of Jean Seznec, was not a theological survival; paganism was recalled by man to serve the cause of humanism, or as Edgar Wind has written, to reconcile pleasure with virtue.[17] From the Renaissance onward, the struggle of the central literary figure is often predominantly a sense of offending against his rational better sense. Under the aegis of Virgil, Dante is the central character of his own work, as Proust was later to be his own Narrator. And the range of mortal experience is the material for both. In a great poem of Petrarch, the poet and Love argue their case before the court of Reason. To Machiavelli a leader is a fallible and not notably virtuous mortal dealing in expedients—a view he derived, as he confirms, from his immersion in classical literature. (Alexander Pope was to write indignantly that "the politic Florentine Nicholas Machiavel affirms that a man needs but to believe himself a hero to be one of the best."[18]) Hamlet, a virtuous prince, a leader born, is an unsurpassed anti-hero, who fatalistically tells us, in the very moment of professing his swordsmanship: "But you would not think how ill all's here about my heart."[19]

All these mutations, nevertheless, existed within a still recognizable frame. And "this huge stage presenteth nought but shows whereon the stars in secret influence comment."[20] Auden's four categories of loss were not yet in receivership, however their meaning might be questioned or resisted by individual writers, or however their persistence might depend, under Puritanism, on hypocrisy. A reference to external events, a deference to the natural and supernatural, a presumption, however altered or ironical, of a larger order, endured in literature if only as belief in the future ages, the future of the earth itself until the nineteenth century, and faltered on into the twentieth. The very names of cultural epochs speak for their links to classical concepts: Renaissance, Augustan, neoclassical. Memory was gaining on history as literary capital; but public action and intimate sentiment were still literarily compatible. Only 150 years ago Walter Scott was able to pay tribute to Jane Austen's mastery of "the exquisite touch on commonplace things," while reserving for himself what he called the Big Wow-Wow.[21]

When Scott offered that tribute, the Big Wow-Wow was increasingly *mal vu*, in literary quarters. Other ideas, or illusions, as Montale might call them, were in literary circulation as to what was fit for history and what for memory. Pope had proposed Ridicule as the only corrective for entrenched pomposity; Burns had declared of the Establishment that the man of independent mind, he looks and laughs at all that.[22] Byron had declared, of attacks on the profanity of his work, "So much the better. I may stand alone, But would not change my free thoughts for a throne."[23]

No poet is more eloquent than Byron on the change in the poet's views on history and memory, changes that intensified as the nineteenth century drew to its close. Of his own work Byron remarked, "If you must have an epic, there's *Don Juan* for you. I call that an epic: it is an epic as much in the spirit of our day as the *Iliad* was in Homer's. Love, religion, and politics form the argument, and are as much the cause of quarrels now as they were then."[24] The transformations of emphasis in these components are a recurring topic in Byron's work. Out of innumerable examples, a single reference—in this case to Marc Antony—will suffice here.

I have already referred to the contrast between Aeneas's abandonment of Dido and Paris's seduction of Helen; Aeneas chose history, the public over the private. His alliance with Lavinia is a mere political expedient—although indeed Turnus feelingly remarks of it that one would think Trojans, with their experience, might have steered clear of women forever.

During Virgil's lifetime, Marc Antony suffered, in 31 B.C., with the Battle of Actium, the fate reserved for the man inadequate to his heroic destiny: dying like a figure of antique—or Japanese—tragedy. Of this downfall, Woman was the explicit cause. Plutarch in fact describes Cleopatra as being decked out as an image of Venus at her celebrated meeting with Antony. Virgil, in a single phrase, refers to Antony's disgrace, condemning him as a man, victorious in every great challenge, who destroyed himself with illicit lust. By Shakespeare's time, Antony's story was recast as a humanly appealing struggle, in which a strong man forfeits for love his right to the hero's immortality.

By 1823, Byron had this to say about Marc Antony's place in history and in memory:

> If Antony be well remembered yet,
> 'Tis not his conquests keep his name in fashion,
> But Actium lost; for Cleopatra's eyes
> Outbalance all of Caesar's victories.[25]

(Not long after writing these words, Byron was to abandon his own mistress to assist in founding the new Greece. By 1937, an analogous decamping by King Edward VIII with Mrs. Simpson—one of whose several names was, paradoxically, Warfield—inspired an enthusiastic

Calypso song: "It was Love Love Love Love, Love alone / Cause King Edward to leave the throne.")

In Shakespeare, of course, other elected heroes divest themselves of their lustrous burden and throw themselves on the mercy of the court of rampant humanism: Richard II tells his courtiers, "I live with bread, like you; feel want, taste grief, / Need friends. Subjected thus, / How can you say to me, I am a king?"[26] Sensibility was a theme for Renaissance writers as for classical authors, as a power of mutual recognition in human kind. But sensibility as an isolating property had gained, by the Romantic period, such ascendancy that Leopardi in the 1830s was cautioning the Romantic poets on the elevation of subjective feelings over the greater mysteries of existence, in contrast with the ancient writers who preserved a humility before the universe. Leopardi says, "And they, the Romantics, do not realize that it is precisely this great ideal of our time, an intimate knowledge of our own heart, and the analyzing, foretelling, and distinguishing of every minute emotion, in short the art of psychology, that destroys the very illusion without which poetry will be no more."[27]

Leopardi, in early youth a translator of Virgil, who grieved over the inhumanity, as he called it, of the Aeneid's closing scene; Leopardi, whose monument stands beside the supposed tomb of Virgil at the entrance of Naples; Leopardi was the author of "A se stesso," as of the "Infinito." Perhaps it is Leopardi among poets who first fully realizes that hubris, egotism, will drive man to destroy, along with Nature and his own relation to the world, his very relation to mystery and his source of poetry. This is a theme close to Montale, who again invoking the *Aeneid*, makes an ironic comment on fashionable modern disbelief:

There is no Sybil at Cuma as far as I know.
And if there was, no one would be such a fool as to listen to it.
(*Non esiste a Cuma una sibilla*
che lo sappia. E se fosse, nessuno
sarebbe così sciocco da darle ascolto.)[28]

(Montale also wrote a poem on being called up by a broadcasting official who wanted his opinion as to whether Dido would make a good subject for television.)[29]

Disbelief in a greater order produces disbelief in one's own obligations, which is a form of disbelief in oneself. The literature of the nineteenth century is often preoccupied with a redefinition of Duty—that is, with an attempt to set the hero up on his own terms. There is a continuous examination of duty—duty to god, to the greater good, to the object of one's affections; or of the conflict between these and a duty to the new hero, oneself: to one's perception of justice and reason and to a human dignity independent of or opposed to established order. Equilibrium was now re-sited in the self. Under new management. One had become a hero merely by bearing with existence, which was no longer gratefully viewed as a gift of gods. Literally regarded, the daily life of man had become a heroic enterprise in itself.

Virtue, even idealism, might still be present in literature; but modern man in his new isolation must bear his destiny in himself—as Lydgate in *Middlemarch*, an innovative scientist and public benefactor, inspired by a noble humanitarian cause, foundering yet again, let us note, on the triviality of a woman. The pure redeeming female of the novel is in fact explicitly likened to the Virgin Mary. Loss of faith is a prevailing theme: "We are most hopeless who had once most hope," Clough tells us, "We are most wretched that had most believed,"[30] while the contingent forces of godless inchoate darkness were confronted in the novels of Hardy. In literature, disillusion relieved itself in unmasking; and this unmasking, under the name of Realism, was a trail swiftly leading to the self. No deed or sentiment, however lofty, was now exempt from reassessment. While Tolstoy poured scorn on the historic phenomenon of "glory," Baudelaire compared memory to a chest of drawers or a communal grave.[31] Psychiatry was on the scene, a valet for whom there are few heroes. Freud's *Interpretation of Dreams* bears an epigraph from Virgil: "If the gods will not stir for me, I'll rouse all hell."

Literary discreditation of vigor was answered with the more languid genius of introspection: Proust told us what was fit for memory, and the Homeric Ulysses was ironically invoked in the obscure Dubliner. The Idiot had become the Hero.

Of this hero, the poet and writer was himself assuming certain attributes. The poet would address himself to power, to authority, to established ideas as to a phenomenon incapable of virtue. The poet would stand apart and accuse order; he would bear solitary witness. In the nineteenth century, exile, prosecution, and imprisonment—always a feature of the writing life—became common among literary figures: Shelley, Hugo, Flaubert, Baudelaire, Zola, Dostoyevsky. The Idiot was becoming an Outcast; but a heroic outcast, at least to himself. As Victor Brombert says in his *Romantic Prison*, "repressed freedom and poetic inventiveness are intimately related."[32]

With the coming of our own century, the institutions of authority seemed bent on justifying the writer's condemnation—bent on identifying "heroism" with destruction and self-destruction. Nature had been, as the saying goes, "subdued." With the onset of the First World War, the state, and society itself, appeared to embrace disorder, to have gone berserk. The betrayal of the helpless man at arms was excruciatingly reported by the poets of the trenches, and Eliot was to ask, "After such knowledge, what forgiveness?"[33] From now on, if equilibrium was to reside anywhere it was in a private, almost conspiratorial exchange of sensibility. The literary duel to the death is no longer between two warriors—Hector and Achilles, Aeneas and Turnus—but is exemplified in Edwin Muir's beautiful poem "The Combat," in which a monstrous heraldic beast endlessly does battle with an unprepossessing little creature who represents the tenacious surviving shred of our humanity.[34]

Everyman was now the anti-hero—a Pooter, a Prufrock—who was to shamble onstage in the plays of Beckett and later of Pinter, and to perish in a seedy limbo in *Death of a Salesman*; the protagonist of such novels as Graham Greene's *Our Man in Havana*, where the vacuum cleaners of the salesman Wormold are mistaken by the authorities for a global missile crisis.

Not everyone accepted this state of literary affairs. On the shell-shocked terrain between the wars, a great poet of our language struggles to reconcile an ancient concept of nobility with the modern reality, and reported failure in magnificent verse. Yeats was, as he said,

> born into that ancient sect
> But thrown upon this filthy modern tide
> And by its formless spawning fury wrecked.[35]

On the death of the hero he warned us:

> And I am in despair that time may bring
> Approved patterns of women and of men
> But not the self-same excellence again.[36]

Poets were beginning to take the measure of loss, and to wonder if the joke might be on them. In 1936, in his "Letter to Lord Byron," Auden reviewed the disintegration of *literary* order as a party which began brilliantly—as he says, "How we all roared when Baudelaire went fey." As the party progressed, he says:

> . . . alas, that happy crowded floor
> Looks very different; many are in tears:
> Some have retired to bed and locked the door;
> And some swing madly from the chandeliers;
> Some have passed out entirely in the rears;
> Some have been sick in corners; the sobering few
> Are trying hard to think of something new.[37]

Poets had not entirely given up on deeds, in life and work. The young Auden was one of numerous writers to endorse, in Spain, a call to arms—

on behalf of a collective literary hero, the proletariat. For these sporadic revivals of action, Montale—who resigned his library post rather than identify himself with fascism—had no respect. "D'Annunzio," he said, "wrote poetry via his social personality. He was so vain that he even managed to be brave in war. [Poor Aeneas!] But vanity was the driving motive, as it was in the case of André Malraux."[38]

Not the proletariat but Everyman was soon—if briefly—to fill the hero's role; and Day Lewis would write of the dead lying in a blitzed London street "They have made us eat our knowing words, who rose and paid the bill for the whole party."[39]

Along with the rest of us, the poet entered the Orwellian postwar world—the era of mass cult, of a technological supremacy whose ultimate achievement is potential annihilation. The poet's aversion to events is representative but immaterial, it lacks the force even to register in what Montale calls the "*civiltà dell'uomo robot*."[40] Montale, like Eliot, is a poet of the end of the line. Unlike Eliot, he brings no religious belief to the void; and his "divine indifference," as he calls it, is a state very far from the *nil admirari* of Horace, that condition of composed maturity. The scraps of life that make ironic appearance in Montale's verse—slivers of soap, squeezed toothpaste, crumpled wrapping paper—are introduced as fit accessories for the meagre modern soul. Mistrusting most passion and all enthusiasm he tells us to take life in small spoonfuls, in homeopathic doses: "*Non aumentate le dose*."[41] His tone is that of a sage whose knowledge can spare us much useless expenditure of emotion. And when he announces—with no little egotism—that he has "Lived at five per cent of capacity," one feels that anyone attempting a larger percentage would be making a *brutta figura*.[42] Far from Virgil's "ocean roll of rhythm," as Tennyson called it, Montale's is a voice lowered so as to cause the auditor to cup his ear.[43] Although sound is measured and essential in every syllable of his verse, Montale—who was a highly trained and knowledgeable musician—is rarely a musical poet. He is aphoristic, but laconic. His poetry is a level gaze at life.

Montale has decreed public events as fit only for history. What then is fit for memory? One of his briefest and most beautiful poems is called "Memory."[44] Memory, he says, was a literary genre before writing was invented and already had a stench of death. Living memory, he says, is immemorial, evanescent, and its content is a secret candor. Not every writer would agree that lofty ideals have entirely passed away from human possibility, or that one may not hope to encounter in literature qualities greater than our own, as we sometimes do in life. In our era, live heroes are often writers themselves—dissidents, prisoners of conscience. The very phrase "our hero" speaks for whatever in the human spirit anciently hungers after revelations and for exemplars (even if exemplars are sanitized nowadays in gibberish as "role-models.") The Aristotelian ideal, that human life "take possession of the beautiful" and live nobly if briefly rather than prolong a commonplace existence is identified by Werner Jaeger as "the sense of heroism through which we feel the classical world most closely akin to ourselves."[45] Mystery remains; and no one can really explain why a multitude outside the Duomo of Milan should break into "oceanic applause" at the sight of a poet's coffin.

Montale has said that every illusion is matched by its disillusion. Yet illusion is the very nature of art. Proust speaks of the historic figures who owe their stature to the illusory magic of literature. Yeats says that civilization itself is "manifold illusion" and that man,

> Despite his terror cannot cease
> Ravening through century after century,
> Ravening, raging and uprooting that he may come
> Into the desolation of reality.[46]

What then of the prospect for art in this nuclear-fearing, overpopulated, polluted, and dehumanized world? Where men and women speak of themselves as case histories or as some inferior mechanism that must adapt itself to all-powerful technology—which can be "perfection" as no human being can be (according to Rilke). Where there is no time for spiritualizing events into legends of honoring gestures. Where Nature, in Montale's words, has withdrawn into the personal myth of the poet; and the poet himself, in Auden's limbo of lost contexts, is a repository of sentiments and sensations that arise like vapor from the deeds of others, lacking even, in our mass culture, the dignity and refreshment of solitude. Even if the specter of an imponderable finality should be exorcised, it seems not impossible that great art may wither away, and that the dynasty of great poets who have nourished our thought for so many centuries is already dying out.

Virgil's *Aeneid* has been called a prolonged literary allusion to Homer. It was Virgil whom Dante chose as his spiritual and literary companion. Crowned with the laurel on the capital of Rome, Petrarch chose the theme of his address from Virgil. In accepting, from detention, his Nobel award, Solzhenitsyn—who had inhabited and described the circles of hell—took his text from Dostoyevsky: "Beauty will save the world."[47] Eugenio Montale's Nobel address was called, "Is Poetry Still Possible?"—poetry, which he has called a pebble, a grain of sand. His address ended with characteristically inconclusive words—which will serve as my own conclusion this evening:

> Not only poetry, but the entire world of artistic expression as it calls itself has entered a crisis indivisible from the human condition, from our life as humane beings, and our conviction or at least illusion of privileged existence as the only creatures who hold themselves masters of their fate and bearers of a destiny no organism can boast. It is therefore useless to ask ourselves what will be the fate of the arts. It would be as if asking whether the man of the future—a future so remote from our conception—will resolve the tragic contradictions in which we have increasingly struggled since the dawn of creation; and whether, by such an epoch, some unimaginable man would still be capable of talking to himself.[48]

2. THE DEFENSE OF CANDOR

If all philosophy is an argument with Plato, as is sometimes claimed, all poetry might be seen as an effort to regain the immediacy of Homer. Literature, like philosophy, is concerned with truth. But the nature of poetry—of literature—extends beyond intellectual enquiry. It engages all human perception, intuitive, rational, mystical, spontaneous, or reflective. It proposes no outcome. It not merely enhances understanding, but is in itself a synthesis. Poets have been at pains to explain this to critics throughout the ages, but their words are unnecessary to lovers of poetry and have been disregarded by critics: The judgment of great poetry, said Whitman, "is as the sun falling around a helpless thing."[49]

In the previous lecture I quoted Montale's observation that memory existed as a literary genre before writing was invented [Ed.: See note 44]. Articulation is an aspect of human survival, not only in its commemorative and descriptive function, but in relieving the human soul of incoherence. In so far as expression can be matched to sensation and event, human nature seems to retain consciousness.

In a sense Realism itself is a means of spiritualizing experience. And a civilized society, forced back to the wall of essentials, called upon the coherence and redemption that a great articulation might provide. That appeal, for poets, is unimaginable in any crisis we might now face.

By introducing this talk with a reference to the indirection that has pervaded Western literature since the time of Homer, I don't intend a tour of familiar theoretical ground. As in my previous talk, I should like to illustrate, through literature itself, the consciousness of writers towards the revelatory or dissembling powers of language. Their commentary is for the most part embedded in their work; it is not theory but practical illustration. Recognition and exposure are present in it, but the artistic purpose is always to return, through language, to essentials, to reclaim truth. In the greatest poets, truth can be found, in Tennyson's phrase, "often flowering often in a lonely word."[50] So that, as Heidegger says of Homeric Greek, "We are directly in the presence of the thing itself, not first in the presence of a mere word-sign."[51] As Coleridge said of Shakespeare's language, it becomes the instrument that makes the changeful god felt in the river, the lion and the flame.[52]

I believe that Heidegger endorsed the tracing of the word *logos* to the harvest, to a gathering of crops. Similarly the Accademia della Crusca—the authority that has reigned over Italian language—takes its name from the sorting of grain from chaff, the sifting of good language from bad; it has a sieve as its emblem. (Unfortunately, the Crusca has in its turn become a symbol for stuffiness.) In the case of *logos*, the word is held, by some philosophers, to refer to the gathering not only of crops but of fruit. A Greek friend of mine proposes a still more direct connection of *logos* to the collecting of *olives*. And there is something compelling in the idea of the word as a small firm pungent fruit, with a hard pit at its center.

Auden's celebrated assertion that Poetry makes nothing happen first appeared, in February 1939, in his memorial poem for Yeats who had died in the previous month.[53] Thirty-odd years before that, Yeats himself had stated that he did not write to affect opinion, but—in his words—to give "emotions expression for my own pleasure. [Otherwise] all would be oratorical and insincere. If we understand our own minds, and the things that are striving to utter themselves through our minds, we move others, not because we have understood or thought about those others, *but because all life has the same root*."[54]

In its preoccupation with the root of life, language has special responsibilities. The visual arts and music are an aesthetic appeal to senses of immediate perception, whatever subsequent impressions they make elicit. But language is the medium through which we all deal continually in daily life. Language, whether as daily speech or transcribed, must be formulated and decoded. Its deviations from true meaning are peculiarly exposed, and some of them fall into familiar categories under ancient names. Yet there are always new variations on impostures, adapted to the receptivity of the times. The multiple possibilities for *valid* approaches to truth through language are themselves increasingly circuitous, and increasingly insistent in their successive claims to be "definitive." In repudiating such pretensions from the realists, Flaubert said, "There is no 'true.' There are merely different ways of perceiving."[55] In considering tonight some of these different avenues toward truth I want to comment on special difficulties that have overtaken "the lonely word" in recent generations, one of the most drastic of those difficulties being reflected in the word's no longer being lonely but found in agglomerations.

To take, as Leopardi does, the familiar Homeric point of departure, is to accept that literary indirection set in early. We have whole schools of explication on this theme. Last lecture I quoted Werner Jaeger's view that the advent of Christianity reinforced rather than introduced the separation of aesthetic literary values from functional ones [Ed.: See note 12]. Norman Douglas, irreverent pagan, says of the Greek Anthology that:

> In the older epigrams, there is present that eye for detail, that touch of earth—bitter or sweet. Slowly it fades away. Even before the commencement of the Christian era concrete imagery tends to be replaced by abstractions. The process was never arrested. The Christians could not allow these things of earth, dear to pagans, to be of much account. They looked inwards, guiding their conduct no longer in relation to tangible objects but to an intangible postulate; and so attained ghostly values. A kind of spiritual dimness had begun to creep over the world.[56]

Douglas felt that even in the translation of classical texts there is some "Anglo-Saxon or Teutonic ferment that produces a saccharine deposit. The mischief has its roots in our gothic distrust of clean thinking." To Douglas, Walter Pater himself was "a noble exponent of the diabetic school. By some alchemy, everything he wrote became charged with a sugary infiltration."[57]

Consciousness is the paradox of human error. Intelligence makes it possible, at least, for Man to establish in retrospect the instant at which they went off the rails; and many institutions and careers have been raised on minute study of our derailments. What is not possible is to resume the collective journey. It is left for a few indigent artists to resume the route on foot. Through art we can feel, as well as know, what we have lost; in art, as in dreams, we can occasionally retrieve and re-experience it. Through art, we can respond ideally to truth, as we cannot in life. It is possible, from time to time, through inspired language, to strike the note of immemorial immediacy.

Immediacy of language is not always or necessarily simplicity. Valéry says that of two words, one must choose the lesser.[58] But we do not always have a lesser word that will meet our need. Heidegger describes the properties of ancient language as distinct and distinguished. Spontaneous directness of oral expression, and simplicity as an instrument of considered language, are different things: a man or woman articulating urgent emotion is not acting under the same impetus as a writer who, from a pondered vocabulary, chooses for best effect and excludes excess. However, urgency does generate a compulsion to truth—just as discursiveness can be an index of falsehood—and veracity tends to express itself with an eminent simplicity—to rise, as it were, to occasion.

In the spring of 1940, when France was falling, Churchill's address to the British nation opened with the words, "The news from France is very bad."[59] A brief sentence of measured sounds, almost entirely composed of words of one syllable. A few years earlier, Churchill had drafted the king's speech of abdication, which (somewhat paradoxically in the circumstances) began with the following sentence: "At last I am able to say a few words of my own."[60] Again, a brief, balanced sentence of single syllables, almost entirely composed of words of Anglo-Saxon or at least non-Latin derivation. In both these instances, a masterful simplicity, a noble difference, gives force and inevitability to seemingly commonplace words. The space has been cleared for them. Dignity and candor are indivisible, and there is a sense of humility before the event; of the self subdued. The occasion and its articulation are at one.

Without diminishing the merits and advantages of brevity, however, literature cannot be looked on as a competition to employ as few words as possible. Rather it is a matter of seeking accurate words to convey a state of mind and imagination. And of deploying words so that tone, context, and sound are ideally combined, without any show of contrivance. That is the proper and agonizing business of literature, in which much of the writer's sufferings originate: "the intolerable wrestle with words and meanings," as Eliot called it.[61] Every writer who is serious about his craft experiences this sense of professing pure meaning with unworthy words. Flaubert told George Sand:

> When I come upon a bad assonance or a repetition in one of my sentences, I'm sure I'm floundering in the false. By dint of searching I find the proper expression, which was always the *only* one, and which is, at the same time, harmonious. The word is never lacking when one possesses the idea. Is there not in this precise fitting of parts, something eternal, like a principle? If not, why should there be a relation between the right word and the musical word? Or why should the greatest compression of thought always result in a line of poetry?"[62]

Great practitioners of language have supplied new words and new usages when, in the literal sense, words failed them. In most cases we echo their innovations unthinkingly, because they satisfy, they meet the case. At other times they bear the maker's seal so distinctly that they can't be uttered without a mental nod in the author's direction. And then there are inventions that cannot be appropriated. When Shakespeare speaks of the "painful warrior, famous'd for fight," or of "fleeting Clarence," or of "the hearts that spaniel'd me at heels," we take his meaning perfectly, but the invention lapses with a single use.[63] In any case these great innovators cannot provide a pattern for lesser talents. Magnitude, as Jacques Barzun says, creates its own space.[64]

More usually, the writer works with words in common use, developing as great a range as possible. Some will bring the whole weight of language to bear. Dr. Johnson said that he could have compiled his dictionary from Bacon's works alone.[65] For the imaginative writer, words are the measure of talent—to an extent not necessarily true for writers dealing in information and ideas. The intentions of a novelist or poet are of course important, but he must be judged on talents of expression that may not be commensurate with them. The intentions of a historian or a critic, on the other hand, necessarily form the basis of our ultimate judgment of his writings, whatever his abilities or deficiencies of communication. The ear of the imaginative writer is ideally tuned to the highest sensitivity, and his method of transcription is perhaps somewhat misleadingly called style. Asked to justify the employment of "fine allusions, bright images, and elegant phrases," Dr. Johnson responded with what might be considered a definition of style: "Why sir, all these ornaments are useful, because they obtain an easier reception for the truth."[66] It is a recurring error of criticism, I think, to treat "style" as an insubstantial literary contrivance distinct from the author's so-called "material."

I have called this talk "The Defense of Candor" because the writer's vigilance over language and his consciousness of its erosion and abuse is a theme running through literature, an indirect commentary, often benign but taking the form of exposure of pretension. I don't refer to satire exclusively, although the English language has been notably congenial to satire—Satire, according to Byron, is the only weapon that doesn't rust in the British climate.[67] In Pope's view, ridicule was the sole corrective for the inveterate offender: "O sacred weapon, left for truth's defence, / Sole dread of folly, vice, and insolence."[68] However, the aspect I would most like to draw attention to here is rather that satire is much less the literary desire to hold offenders up to salutary public scorn than to depict character and eternal human characteristics. In literature this portrayal turns on a use of words, and often of a single word; in the novel it is most frequently rendered through qualities of speech, as in this very modern observation from George Eliot's *Middlemarch*:

> Mr. Vincy felt sure it would not be long before he heard of Mr. Featherstone's demise. The felicitous word "demise," which had seasonably occurred to him, had raised his spirits even above their usual evening pitch. The right word is always a power. Considered as a demise, old Featherstone's death assumed a merely legal aspect, so that Mr. Vincy could tap his snuff box over it and be jovial, without even an intermittent affectation of solemnity.[69]

The novelist's defense of candor could be well illustrated through this book alone. I know of no work of fiction other than Proust in which character is so consistently illustrated through language. I confess I was tempted to give this talk exclusively on *Middlemarch*. Concern with words and sounds runs through the book as a conscious theme—there is even a scene of a grammar lesson given by a mother to her child. There is Mrs. Bulstrode, who felt that "in using the superior word 'militate' she had thrown a noble drapery over a mass of particulars."[70] There is Mr. Casaubon who, even in saying "Yes," manages with a "peculiar pitch of voice [to make] the word half a negative"[71]—and a drop of whose blood is said to show, under a magnifying glass, nothing but "semicolons and parentheses."[72] There is Mr. Trumbull, "an amateur of superior phrases"[73] with a way of saying, "'It commences well.' (Things never began with Mr. Borthrop Trumbull: they always commenced . . .)."[74] George Eliot, referring in this book to a new self-consciousness in language, speaks of what she calls "the lusty ease" of Fielding's "fine [eighteenth-century] English," which seems, she says, as if delivered from an armchair on a proscenium, while her own contemporaries and she herself produce what she calls "thin and eager chat, as if delivered from a campstool in a parrot-house."[75]

Writers have immemorially delighted in puncturing pretensions of speech. One need but recall the poem of Catullus, "Arrius," or Hamlet with Polonius.[76] It seems strange to find George Eliot lamenting the decline of English at a time when fluency and genius of expression appear unsurpassed in our literature. However, the industrial revolution of the nineteenth century was bringing about what might be called an industrial revolution in thought and language, and an accelerated change in the long evolution of formal speech. The treatment of individual speech in literature first appears in English in the medieval rendering of *types*—especially of rustics—through the medium of vernaculars. There was also a special tone of language for genres of literature—as the tone of the epic is different from that of romance. It is with the development of the drama, and departure from the rules of rhetoric, that men and women begin to speak with their own personalities.

This was a humanistic assumption of individual responsibility, as we have continued, in theory at least, to consider it. Each person's words, in literature as in life, are accepted as a revelation of their nature, and an index of the measure of responsibility they were prepared to assume for it. As Gabriel observes to Satan: "Evasion is rooted in fear as responsibility arises from conviction."[77] The sense of individual responsibility through words has proved very hard to maintain—it seems that the medieval forms of class responsibility provided a shelter that has been sought ever since through linguistic embellishment and evasion. William Empson wrote of the seventeenth century that what was said of the Emperor Augustus in relation to Rome might be said of Dryden and the English language: that he found it brick and left it marble.[78] This, of course, was not necessarily an improvement. Another great change sets in with the nineteenth century. Along with the transforming powers of technology there came a stronger tendency to renounce personal in favor of generalized or expert opinion, and to evade self-knowledge through use of abstractions; a wish to believe in some process more generalized or efficient than human feeling. By the 1870s Trollope was able to introduce the following dialogue as conversation at a fashionable party. Speaking of a friend, Phineas Finn says to a young woman:

> ". . . . He is the most abstract and concrete man I know.
> "Abstract and concrete!"
> "You are bound to use adjectives of that sort now, Miss Palliser, if you mean to be anybody in conversation."[79]

There was also the associated new phenomenon of mass communications and mass advertising—that is, of new words not spontaneously but speciously brought into being as a means of profitably controlling human impulse. We have a young man of Middlemarch, for instance, renouncing use of the word "superior" because, as he says, "There are too many *superior* teas and sugars these days. Superior is getting to be shopkeepers' slang."[80] That scene is set in 1831, although of course *Middlemarch* was written several decades later. In 1834, in *Le Père Goriot*, the residents of the pension Vauquer take up the suffix "-rama," which has been recently publicized in connection with the invention of diorama; "-rama" is facetiously appended to every other word while the fad lasts. Observations of the kind abound in Dickens, along with an extraordinary prescience for the dehumanizing properties of all jargon, particularly of bureaucratic jargon—for instance, he sets his Circumlocution Office in Bleeding Heart Yard, and prophesies it will lead to Britannia's downfall.

I have spoken of a renunciation of independent and eccentric views that accompanied the growth of mass culture. In aesthetic matters this has also been encouraged by an assumption of critical authority that, in the words of one modern critic, will "deal expertly" with literature and other arts, relieving readers of time-consuming burdens of private choice. While commentary and scholarly attention have always existed toward literature, and always will, a new body of attitudes has developed that seems to seek to neutralize the very directness to life which is nurtured by art. This phenomenon is notably one of explication rather than comprehension—the concept of art as a discipline to be contained within consistent laws, the seductive promise of a technology to be mastered by those who will then be equipped to dictate taste. There is the wish to dictate a view rather than accept the submission required by art—a submission akin to generosity or love, which evokes the individual response rather than the authorized one. Art is not technology, it is an endless access to revelatory states of mind, a vast extension of living experience, and a way of communing with the dead. An intimacy with truth, through which, however much instruction is provided and absorbed, each of us must pass alone.

The degradation of language in the extreme versions of these explicatory approaches to the arts should be the first concern of anyone wishing to penetrate and rehabilitate them. The so-called clinical approach necessitates a dehumanized and labored vocabulary. (A reputation becomes "canonical status," a life together is a "symbiotic relationship" and so on. And I have even heard at Princeton works of literature referred to as systematized narratology.) There seems to be little awareness of the lesson that lies in language psychiatry. While certain of the academic and journalistic mills grind small over "the creative impulse," the impulses of critics have attracted less attention. Yet the restless Unconscious of the critical body deserves some exploration, if only to probe its effects on the life of the imagination, and to discover why critics of this kind so seldom step aside to allow art to speak, inimitably, for itself—art often appearing to be regarded by them as "mere material" for dissection and classification.

Much of this encroachment of abstract language derives from a modern inability for wholeness; a modern incapacity for synthesis. While it poses as a higher seriousness, abstraction is perhaps another stage in the long attempt to neutralize the mysteries that are inimical to human vanity. Inimical, that is, to self-knowledge. Seneca, writing to a friend about the beauty of literature, remarks that when a literary critic goes through the same book, he emerges mainly with the news that Ennius filched the idea from Homer and that Virgil filched it from

Ennius, and so on. He says, "To my mind, no one lets humanity down so much as these people who study knowledge as if it were some sort of technical skill."[81] One could cite a thousand such observations from every period of literature—Shakespeare is full of them, as when Horatio remarks that Hamlet will need marginal notes to follow the speech of Osric, or when Richard II speaks of thoughts that are so "intermix'd with scruples that they set the word itself against the word."[82] Chesterton tells us that "the north is full of tangled things and texts and aching eyes; / and gone is all the innocence of anger and surprise."[83]

I think the defense of candor intensified to meet new incursions when they showed their new modern power. The rumble of abstractions runs through much of nineteenth- and twentieth-century literature as a threat to individual being. We believe in the crushing weight of Mr. Gradgrind's dreadful FACTS, as, alas, we do not believe in Dickens's redemption of this linguistic sinner. In a section of Ford Madox Ford's *Parade's End*, during a love scene between two principals who are sitting by a fireside, we are told that in the same room, "A Mr. Jegg and a Mrs. Haviland were sitting together in the window-seat. From time to time, Mr. Jegg used the word, 'inhibition.'" The love scene proceeds by the fire, and then we're told: "Behind their backs the fire rustled. Across the room, Mrs. Jegg said, 'The failure to coordinate.'"[84]

This is as much a modern background as the proclamations about cows and pigs that arise from the country fair in *Madame Bovary* while a love scene takes place in a room above; or the incongruously frivolous offstage music heard in the *Tales of Hoffman* as a murder takes place. However, one might now feel that the chorus of dehumanized expression has prevailed, while the word expressive of the root of life can be heard only in an occasional aside, or through the din.

3. POSTERITY: "THE BRIGHT REVERSION"

My title, "The Bright Reversion," is drawn from a verse in Byron's dedicatory preface to *Don Juan*:

> He that reserves his laurels for posterity
> (Who does not often claim the bright reversion)
> Has generally no great crop to spare it, he
> Being only injured by his own assertion.
> And although here and there some glorious rarity
> Arise like Titan from the sea's immersion,
> The major part of such appellants go
> To—God knows where—for no one else can know.[85]

The phrase "the bright reversion" was taken, in turn, by Byron from one of his idols, Alexander Pope, who asks, "Is there no bright reversion in the sky / For those who greatly think, or bravely die?"[86]

The premise of artistic posterity is generally that the work that retains posthumous meaning has worth. As soon as one begins to examine it, however, posterity emerges as one of the larger mysteries of the largely mysterious phenomenon of art. The greatest mystery being why art should exist at all and why a few beings should be capable of creating it, and still fewer of doing so—always given the lottery of survival—with enduring power. Selective, elusive, and unpredictable in the extreme, literary posterity has, as such, been explicitly celebrated, wooed, or disdained by centuries of writers in innumerable works. One finds early examples of poets superstitiously exorcising the vengeance of time—for example, Homer forthrightly claims that future ages shall know of the sufferings of his heroes; whereas Virgil, appropriating that very line from Homer, inserts the word "perhaps." The title of this lecture might well have been "Perhaps." Over and over one finds writers referring in their work to their chances with posterity—whether to stake their claim with future ages, to repudiate any such ambition, or to acknowledge—like Milton—an unworthy preoccupation with Fame. Posterity is a kind of Tenth Muse, hovering ironically over the other Nine.

Byron himself made, in a variety of moods, a wide variety of comments on posterity. *Don Juan* is full of sardonic comments on the theme. Of himself he says fatalistically that "What I write I cast upon the stream / To swim or sink. I have had at least my dream."[87] With hindsight we may think more appropriate his lines in *Childe Harold*, written only slightly earlier:

> But there is that within me shall tire
> Torture and Time, and breathe when I expire;
> Something unearthly, which they deem not of,
> Like the remember'd tone of a mute lyre.[88]

The Romantics were often at special pains to forestall oblivion by assuring the future that they expected nothing from it—as if Posterity were some rich old uncle with a fortune to dispose of. Keats was one of many who proposed their own epitaph: "Here lies one whose name was writ in water." Stendhal wished to be remembered as one who loved Shakespeare, Mozart, and Cimarosa.[89] Remembrance was in the air. In a letter about his imminent death Keats said, "If I should die, I have left no immortal work behind me—nothing to make my friends proud of my memory—but I have loved the principle of Beauty in all things, and if I had time, I would have made myself remembered."[90] Leopardi, shortly before his death, wrote that, "despite the fine title 'Collected Works' given by the bookseller to my volume, I have never accomplished anything real. I have only made attempts, believing them preludes. But my career has done no further."[91]

When Leopardi wrote that, he was living at Naples and producing possibly the greatest of all his poems, "La Ginestra," a poem about posterity inspired by the yellow flowers of the broom growing on the bleak lava of the Vesuvius—a symbol at once of the transience of man, the replenishment and renewal of nature, and the infinity of the universe. The poem refers to the cities of Pompeii and Herculaneum whose posterity, artistic and otherwise, ranks among the weirdest of all survivals. In a passage of the poem that might deal directly with our own era, the poet apostrophizes his own nineteenth century with its proclamations of "progress":

Here look and see yourself, you preposterous century,
That going backwards calls this progress,
Ignoring all the arduous knowledge of past ages.[92]

He goes on to say that even the intelligentsia feel obliged to pay tribute to their era simply because they themselves inhabit it—while sometimes expressing doubts behind their hands. Leopardi says, "I shall not go underground with that disgrace upon me; but shall proclaim my scorn of this century with my last breath. Although I know that Oblivion presses heaviest on those who will not celebrate their times."[93]

In fact, no literary name is more celebrated in Italy today than that of Leopardi. And it seems there is scarcely any common factor, even that of genius, in literary fame. Why indeed do we feel a need for literary posterity? Horace said that the strong men who lived before Agamemnon passed into oblivion because they lacked a sacred poet (although as Montale remarked, memory was a literary genre before writing was invented.)[94] There are now all too many other ways of recording the deeds of strong men; but the need is still felt of—so to speak—the sacred poet, to transmit sensations and sentiments. Why this is so might be the theme of many lectures. It has been exquisitely dwelt upon by Proust in the concluding section of his work where he treats the distinctions of supposed "reality," the sharp image, with the successive states of being and impression that constitute—even if summarized in few words—the immortality of human memory.

The human wish that something of our existence should linger to inform later generations is at its best one of our larger desires—the reciprocity between the living and the dead. What we frankly call the pleasure of ruins must derive from the simultaneous reassurance and confirmation of shared mortality evoked by evidence of past existence, and of the helplessness and power of human knowledge, the urge of our forebears to strike the heart of some unknown future soul. All this is perhaps most of all manifest in the lonely word: in Shakespeare's imperative desire to commemorate his love—as the sonnet says, "that in black ink my love may still shine bright."[95] Or Byron pronouncing that

> Words are things; and a small drop of ink
> Falling like dew upon a thought, produces
> That which makes thousands, perhaps millions, think.
> 'Tis strange, the shortest letter which man uses
> Instead of speech, may form a lasting link of ages.[96]

Posterity has been used by writers as a present threat: Chateaubriand confronting Napoleon, at the risk of his life, with the reminder that Nero railed in vain, because Tacitus was born within the Empire; in our time, Miłosz warning the oppressor, "You who harmed a simple man, do not feel secure; For a poet remembers."[97]

There is also the wish to share pleasure. A contemporary of David Garrick's composed a piece of music for the cello—that being the instrument, with lower range as well as middle register, most closely approximating the human voice—to render the inflections of Garrick's delivery of Hamlet's soliloquy. (I've heard this performed, and uncanny it is.)

Posterity devolves on those who have not sought it. Twenty years ago or more, there appeared in the *New Yorker* a tiny poem by James Kirkup, an English poet living in Japan, addressed to a Japanese poet of the turn of this century, Ochi-Ai Naobumi:

> You said if you could find one person
> Who had let himself be touched by your poems
> You would die happy.
> I have come too late to tell you
> How your brief poem moved me
> With its modesty and longing.[98]

This is the only afterlife of which we have evidence—the transmission of human experience and thought. The wish to distinguish poets and writers who have power is an immemorial attempt to touch future ages. Byron speaks of conferring laurels. The laureled poet was formally recognized as the vessel through which man's voice might be transmitted to the future. Crowned in ancient Greece at the Pythian Festival, honored in Rome with the sacred leaves, as Virgil calls them—the wreath that on the poet's brow, according to Horace, admitted him to the company of gods; even while those very leaves commemorated the inability of Apollo to consummate his desire. The laurel set the poet not so much apart from others as above others—acknowledging him greater than usual beings and—to borrow Montale's phrase—fit for memory. Not entirely an illusion, perhaps. The little branch of laurel served so long as a symbol of immortality that its leaves still rustle through our conversation. In Italy the laurel has maintained a spell second only to the halo as a persistent symbolic presence in literature and in the poet's consciousness.

In 1341 Petrarch was crowned with the poet's laurel on the Capitol of Rome; he chose for his address of acceptance a text from Virgil, a text which, with echoes of Lucretius, exalts the private realm, the originality of talent and its contingent loneliness. (*Sed me Parnassi deserta per ardua dulcis raptat amor.*[99]) Of his crown Petrarch subsequently said, "This laurel gained for me no knowledge, but rather much envy"[100]—an observation echoed by Saul Bellow in a recent comment on his own Nobel award: "The prize was a pain in the neck."[101]

The laurel continues to haunt the modern Italians. Guido Gozzano, whose short life ended in 1916, is, as it were, a modern Italian poet marking a transition, a rupture with formality. His beautiful long poem, "Signorina Felicità," describes the idyll of a young man of intellect with a country girl—a girl whose total ignorance is highly approved by the poet. (It is a poem to drive any feminist up the wall.) One day the girl shows the young man her family's attic, crammed with outmoded furniture, discarded mattresses, pots and pans, mildewed engravings. Among the engravings, there is a series of "distinguished persons," including a portrait of Tasso. And the girl, knowing nothing either of the laurel or of Tasso, asks why those absurd old codgers are wearing cherry leaves on their heads. The young man laughs, but laughing thinks, "So this is glory—a dim corridor, some outworn furniture, a bad likeness in a cheap frame, inscribed with the mildewed name of Torquato Tasso."[102]

Of the laurel, Montale, no less than other Italian poets, has much to say. One of Montale's first published poems, written about the time Mussolini came to power, is called "The Lemons," and contrasts the lemon tree favorably with the stately varieties of plant—acanthus, myrtle, boxwood—with which the laureled poets concern themselves.[103] Elsewhere he tells us that a dried laurel isn't even good in the Sunday roast.

For Virgil, it is Apollo himself who plucks the poet by the ear. Montale describes his muse as a ragged scarecrow flapping in an obscure vineyard.[104] This proclaimed diffidence is in its way a bravado about glory and posterity.

While it's tempting to reverse the issue of posterity, to see it as defining what we collectively require from art, the theme will not resolve itself in such coherent terms. It is filled with contradictions not only because different times and societies seek differing forms of recognition, solace, or stimulus, and different fashions or political movements play their role, but because the accidental is a capital force, in posterity as in life. A considerable literature, for instance, has come down to us from the court of tenth-century Japan, the Heian court, the world of Lady Murasaki. That this is almost exclusively written by women stems from the fact that Chinese was the elevated language of the Heian court—an outmoded and mutilated form of Chinese, incomprehensible in China itself. The business and formalities of the Japanese court were carried on in this artificial language by male courtiers and officials, while the court ladies were held unworthy of the distinction. Educated women were thus the repositories of the Japanese language, and their ample leisure allowed certain of them to develop their country's literature.

At times longevity and a large body of work appears to impress a writer on human memory. At others, the public imagination is captured by the tragedy of early or violent death. The writer may outlive his early fame as Swinburne did; like Shelley, he may enter into it with his death. ("Now he knows whether there is a God or no."[105]) He may be honored for his public role—like Solzhenitsyn—or because he was a recluse. Death itself can be a releasing force in enabling the world to realize a loss (as with the case of John Hall Wheelock)—critics who have been fearful of honoring a living writer seem to pluck up courage when they sense he may be entering on his literary afterlife. Writers may be resurrected, so to speak, because they seem to speak for a particular social change—as we now see happening with women writers who give expression or add lustre to the newly liberated consciousness of women. Or a writer may appear to epitomize a national mood by his person, life, and work, or by the nature of his death—as Rupert Brooke for the British public of 1915, when he embodied ideals or illusions of which he has since become the ironically ingenuous symbol.

Rupert Brooke described his own posterity in his poem, "The Soldier" ("If I should die, etc"). At his death of septicemia, during the campaign in the Dardanelles in 1915, Rupert Brooke was buried by night in a foreign field—an olive grove to be precise—in a remote part of the island of Skyros, where his simple grave has been tended and visited by occasional British travelers. In 1979, the *Times* of London reported that a road for trucks had been pushed through that still otherwise inaccessible region, the traffic passing within a foot or so of the poet's grave. As a result of representations from the British government, the road has now been slightly diverted, and the tract of it that passed through Brooke's corner of the foreign field has been allowed to grow over, at least for the present.

It is hard for us to believe now that Wallace Stevens, in his poem "Mozart 1935," could write "We may come back to Mozart."[106] In the impenetrable mystery of posterity there is something of a mirror image of life—of existence itself, with its enigmas and accidental qualities, its moods and recurring fads, its contradictions and inconsistencies that we seek to compress into the rational and discussable forms of our inability to accept our mortality, while incapable of living in a wider context. The ambiguities of our own age toward posterity are not the least bizarre of the mysteries. On the one hand, the industry of oral history, of time capsules, of the hoarding and buying at huge sums of the papers and libraries of writers, the commemorating even of authors' most casual remarks, the assembling of their correspondence, the assiduity for getting writers down on tape or down on paper, or for just getting them down. On the other hand, the neglect and ignorance of past knowledge, the dying out of the study of ancient languages, the contempt or even terror of what is stigmatized "conventional" or "traditional," the obsession with novelty and the up-to-date, possibly at the expense of genuinely fresh talent; the large claims made for artistic anarchy because it is supposedly expressive of our times. The conservation of books, on the one hand; and their accelerating disintegration on the other. One might say the preservation of antique fragments, and the destruction of the Acropolis; the extended lifespan of man, and the threat of nuclear obliteration.

I have spoken previously about art and in particular the articulating of man's fate as a maintaining of the human consciousness. It is in this sense of contributing to human wisdom, liberty, and pleasure that the so-called posterity of an artist—of a writer—rises above mere vanity or an elevated ambition for power. Auden, who wrote that "time . . . worships language"[107] says that "The whole aim of a poet, or any other kind of artist, is to produce something which is complete and will endure without change."[108] Randall Jarrell, in "The Obscurity of the Poet" says that "the poet writes his poem for its own sake, for the sake of that order of things in which the poem takes the place that has awaited it," and he goes on to quote one of the most beautiful passages of Proust—that we enter this life as though carrying a burden of obligations contracted in a former, higher existence, the obligations created by other beings who have contributed to our knowledge and self-knowledge.[109]

Auden writes of "something which is complete." I believe this touches on the question of wholeness to which I referred in "The Defense of Candor" in connection with a modern incapacity for synthesis—a fear of wholeness that reveals itself in a mania for explication, classification, and dissection. However that may be, I think it is generally accepted that an artist hopes at least that his works will outlive him, that they are self-sufficient enough to pass into futurity; an assumption logical enough, since artistic work is presumably intended to give pleasure and interest to as wide an audience as possible.

However, there are and always have been those who repudiated this view. "There is first reconciliation to oblivion"—John Marston.[110] I don't refer to the conjecture or acceptance of oblivion. More strikingly, there are artists for whom, in the words of the Chilean poet Nicanor Parra, "disorder holds its charm." (In a poem called "I take back everything I've said," he asks the reader to burn the book. Why then royalties to quote therefrom?) (*Me retracto de todo lo dicho.*[111]) These are the words of the painter Dubuffet on the theme: "I believe in the utility of oblivion. I should like to see a mammoth statue of Oblivion in the main square of every town, instead of the libraries and museums we see there today. / Let's make a clean sweep of the art of the past! I do my best to make art as if no one had ever made it before. . . . I am an antihumanist."[112]

In calling for the—somewhat paradoxical—monument to Oblivion, Dubuffet is already twenty-eight-hundred years out of date. According to legend, such a monument existed, in the statue to Sardanapulus at Nineveh whose inscription celebrated oblivion. Some might hold that such monuments existed in Dubuffet's own work. These words of Dubuffet, along with much more of the same—all of them with dates of the 1950s and 1960s—appeared in print last year here in connection with a, let's say, monumental exhibition at the Guggenheim Museum, titled Retrospective.[113]

I don't mean to mock Dubuffet—though I think his assertions might bear a little ironic treatment. His desire that forms of art in conflict with his own should be destroyed is perhaps more significant than he perhaps allows. What he feels—or felt—is an aspect of human impulse like any other and not an unfamiliar one. However, he utters these shockers secure—as it were—that what he advocates will not readily come to pass unless in the complete annihilation of our world. There is something of a French tradition here. Proust, taking up analogous views of Baudelaire, says he is shocked enough to find Baudelaire expressing such sentiments, but nothing like as shocked as when he discovers them in Dostoyevsky. Because, Proust says, "at least I know that Baudelaire is not sincere."[114]

Proust is not, of course, accusing Baudelaire of expressing false sentiments but acknowledging a gulf between sentiment and an utter commitment such as nihilism—though even nihilism has its tradition—a distance between an environment in deadly earnest, and one in which artists and poets have traditionally explored sensation in the knowledge that no such exercise need be conclusive. Not for nothing was Dubuffet in youth a Voltairean and a friend, even a disciple, of Raymond Queneau. At a relatively early stage Dubuffet published two volumes of his writings—as John Russell remarks, he took care that posterity should be well informed of his desire for Oblivion. (A preferable form of posterity would perhaps be that of Machiavelli as manifested at the conference of scholars held in 1969 at Florence, on commemoration of the five-hundredth anniversary of Machiavelli's death.)

Our own age—the last decades of the twentieth century—has its own peculiar and new paradoxes; the justified assumption of longer life, and greater leisure together with the sense of time cosmically running out. Our disbelief—our lack of complete confidence, at any rate—in posterity, and certainly our incapacity to imagine its forms and attitudes, infect the human mood of the present and the nature of art and work produced. Public acclaim, celebration of the achiever, however fleeting his renown, takes its notorious toll of the artistic spirit and its ability to create. Writers have historically cautioned against this, but they have never had to make themselves heard over such an uproar and such commercial interests, nor to feel that their warnings might count for nothing against so precarious a future. Samuel Johnson who in early youth composed a revelatory poem on this theme called "The Young

Author," wrote in age, "When a man has made celebrity necessary to his happiness, he has put it in the power of the weakest and most timorous malignity."[115] Byron—who was a celebrity indeed—has his say about the "eighty greatest living poets";[116] Leopardi wrote that "Fame, in literature, is sweet when a man nourishes it in silence and solitude as a foundation for new enterprises. But when it is enjoyed in the world and society, it is nothing."[117]

Of the modern loss of this necessity for spiritual silence, perhaps the greatest of all modern deprivations for the life of the mind and imagination—for the soul, as it used to be called—Montale has said: "Only a man who lives in solitude can speak of the fatal isolation we suffer under this inhuman, mass-produced communication. Being in fashion and famous seems now the only accepted role for the contemporary artists . . . and I ask myself where this absurdity will lead us. Personal responsibility demands patience and solitude, and both these factors are dismissed by the modern world."[118]

Some years ago in the time when the executive branch of government still sought sporadically to distinguish this country's poets, I was invited one evening to the apartment of a prominent politician to hear a poet read. The poet had submitted the names of twenty or so friends—mostly other poets—whom he wished to be present. When we arrived we learned that the official who had invited us would not be present, having been detained, as his wife said, "at an important political meeting." This lady then conducted the affair, and our friend the poet read several poems. When he had finished reading, there was a short silence, and the hostess said, "Well, let's get the ball rolling." By which we understood we were supposed to discuss what we had just heard. As no one spoke, she said, "I'll start off. W. H. Auden said that the history of Europe would be exactly the same, wars and persecutions, and so on, if no poem had ever been written and art had never existed."

This time there was a still longer silence. And then Cleanth Brooks, I think it was, said, "Well, it might be just the same. But would it be worth reading?"

PART 2

The Expressive Word

A MIND LIKE A BLADE

Review of Muriel Spark, *Collected Stories I* and *The Public Image*

There are aspects of the obvious that can only be revealed to us by genius. It might, for instance, be said of Franz Kafka that he has enabled even those who have never read a line of his works to say of certain situations, "This is Kafkaesque," and to know what was implied. Something of such a singular view that speaks a truth recognizable even to those who do not explore its origins, may be said to emanate from the works of Muriel Spark.

At this moment, when, in all the arts, novelty is frequently confused with quality, Mrs. Spark's writings demonstrate how secondary—in fact, how incidental—are innovations of style and form to the work of the truly gifted: such innovation is a natural by-product of their originality rather than its main object. When the word "humorous" has little currency in literature or in life, her wit is employed to produce effects and insights only matched in contemporary fiction, in this reviewer's opinion, by the glittering jests of Vladimir Nabokov. At a time when our "tolerance" tends to take the form of general agreement that we are all capable of the worst crimes had we but the conditions for committing them, Mrs. Spark interests herself instead in our capacities for choice and in the use we make of them; and in those forces of good and evil that she picks out, often gleefully, beneath their worldly camouflage.

In all Muriel Spark's work there is a sense of high spirits and of, to use one of her own similes, "a mind like a blade."[1] She does not posture instructively, not does she shade her work to appease reviewers and gladden the hearts of publishing companies: she writes to entertain, in the highest sense of the word—to allow us the exercise of our intellect and imagination, to extend our self-curiosity and enrich our view.

Such are the pleasures to be derived from the first volume of a projected series of Mrs. Spark's collected stories and from her new, short novel. Short-story collections are often criticized as being "uneven"—presumably by those who prize uniformity in art—and it is not likely that these stories, some of them written years apart, should be of identical weight and tone. Mrs. Spark is a writer who has continually sought to develop and enlarge her art and, where necessary, to convulse it. It is precisely this "unevenness," this diversity and range of the stories, that makes the volume extraordinary, for the author is prepared to observe us under any circumstances and to recount her impressions in the form she finds appropriate.

The stories take place in Africa, in Hampstead, on the moon. Some of them hinge on a single crucial incident, other recount a multiplicity of events inexorably brought to their common fulfillment. Several contain a difficult element of the supernatural; others, like the delightful "Alice Long's Dachshunds" and "Daisy Overend," go to the very roots of our nature. These stories—which, with their trains of thought that have been pursued in her novels, can now be viewed within the body of the writer's work—seem at times varied enough to have been written by different authors: yet each is totally, movingly recognizable as hers.

Palinurus in *The Unquiet Grave*, speaks of "the art which is distilled and crystallized out of a lucid, curious and passionate imagination."[2] It is this passionate curiosity that extends the art of Mrs. Spark beyond the detachment that can so readily become its own victim. The uniqueness and secrecy of each soul is fascinating to her: "I found that Jennifer's neurosis took the form of 'same as.' We are all the same, she would assert, infuriating me because I knew that God had made everyone unique."[3] She will not let us vitiate our perceptions with sentiment, or allow us the doubtful refuge of clinical abstractions if we are to encounter the blessed in disguise; we must also recognize those in love with their own good will or with the virtuous sense of their own guilt, those who would have us conform to their own concept of sensibility.

In one of the strongest stories in this collection, "Bang-bang You're Dead," a woman finds herself complimenting a poet on verses she privately considers third-rate. "She did not know then," the author tells us, "that the price of allowing false opinions was the gradual loss of one's capacity for forming true ones."[4] In the same story we are told, "There is no health, she thought, for me, outside of honesty."[5] Mrs. Spark's literary strivings after this form of health can make the efforts of other authors seem as banal as a get-well card. No modern writer has given greater attention to our revelatory turns of phrase, or more richly conjured up the inflections of meaning in our language.

By the same token, her artistry in these stories is scrupulously disciplined. She does not indulge herself in enumerating sensations or cataloguing objects merely because she is aware of them: everything must bear on what she has to tell us. Nor does she seek, as narrator, to establish her own virtue as contrasted with the fallibility of those she writes about. There is no attempt, for example, in the fine first story in the collection, "The Portobello Road," to palliate the stern decision that leads to the narrator's death: if we assume the writer to be human, we must allow her characteristics that will not always please us. In much of the book there is a complex sense of ultimate order, which it may not be entirely fanciful to link to an Edinburgh upbringing.

One reads these brilliant stories with conscious pleasure in the author's fresh, independent gift and in the vitality of her intelligence. And with a sharing of her own delight.

In *The Public Image*, Mrs. Spark continues to sound deep waters. Annabel Christopher, a minor film actress who has suddenly, freakishly, become a star, has settled in Rome with her husband, Frederick, and their baby, in order to make a film there. Frederick, a seedy screenwriter, has brought his hanger-on, Billy, with whom he has shared the ever-widening periphery of Annabel's success. When Frederick goes mad with envy and kills himself (on the spot "where they have placed the martyrdom of St. Paul"), leaving a set of letters and circumstances intended to destroy his wife's career, Annabel at first reacts within her public image.[6] She is tempted to perpetuate the false identity built up for her by press agents and journalists, to suppress the facts of the suicide, and buy off the blackmailing Billy. In a series of flashbacks of ironic cast, we trace the events that have led Annabel to Rome and into temptation. At the end of the book, when repudiating the tyranny of what others wish her to be, she simply states the truth—unleashes it, one might say, on those around her—we follow her out of a courtroom and into a crowd where, divested of her public image, she goes unrecognized and free.

Throughout this parable Mrs. Spark employs her sense of actions that, accumulating over years, are at last irresistibly telescoped into a liberating calamity. As elsewhere in her work, she heightens suspense not by withholding facts but by causing us to speculate as to their effects on her characters. In this book, once again, suffering is being obliged to submit to those who would have us predictable and alike. Set in the film world, this is the most film-like of her novels—interiors and objects are distinct and significant, people are sharply captured in their moment of emergency. There is an endless, dreadful housewarming, a chorus of genially vacant neighbors, and a child who does not so much blurt out truth as take a fiendish satisfaction in her own guilelessness.

The equivocal nature of public curiosity, and its infringements of private life, are depicted here in their subtlety and their brutality. Those who speak for sanity—the wordless baby, a film director, a doctor, Frederick's Italian mistress, and ultimately Annabel herself—appear not as total embodiments of reason and justice but surprising or irresolute, as in life. We are not required to approve of everything in Annabel, but to recognize her experience and the necessity of her choice. Similarly, the author does not find it necessary to "punish" the loathsome Billy: his punishment is to be that way.

In telling us this taut contemporary tale, Mrs. Spark displays all the directness and complexity of her art, and her poet's accuracy of thought and word. Here is a remarkable writer stimulating us with her "harsh merriment," and with her splendid chartings of human dissimilarity.[7]

REVIEW OF JEAN RHYS, *QUARTET*

The reappearance of this first novel by Jean Rhys, originally published in 1928 (with, in England, the title *Postures*), is the latest dividend from a revival of interest in Miss Rhys that has recently produced new editions of her other novels. This early work opens the theme—developed in *Voyage in the Dark* and reaching full power in the beautiful *Wide Sargasso Sea*—of an imaginative, susceptible nature destroyed by the assertive, unyielding world.

The art of Jean Rhys derives from an acute, even morbid, sensibility and perception. It is the private sensations experienced and exchanged by her characters that give her novels meaning; and by extension this is her view of life. Her heroines (there are no heroes) embody not so much a capacity for suffering as a thwarted capacity for joy. Irony is never absent, even when the author is most deeply in sympathy. These attributes, which exclude any ready social message and must be judged independently on quality, in general evoke uneasiness and hostility in contemporary critics; and one may doubt whether Miss Rhys would be receiving the current highly deserved critical acclaim if her works were now being published for the first time. But a literary durability of forty years can apparently allay the insecurity of even the most assiduous avant-gardists, and readers who have always admired Miss Rhys will be pleased that news of her gifts has at last filtered through to that quarter.

Miss Rhys, who is now eighty-one and lives in Devon, is at present at work on an autobiographical volume [Ed.: Rhys died in 1979]. Her novels themselves, while they cannot be said to deal with an identical character, are progressively concerned with the incapacity of an intelligent woman to defend her affections. A surprising quotation on the jacket of *Quartet* finds Miss Rhys's work "empty of self-pity"; yet for me her power lies in the very transition of self-pity into literature—a feat of artistic strength seldom accomplished even by poets.

The heroine of *Quartet*, Marya Zelli, is an English girl living in Paris who finds herself destitute when her shifty, shiftless Polish husband is imprisoned for petty crime. She is taken in by an English couple, the Heidlers, who are ringleaders of an ingrown group of well-to-do expatriates. This is the English-speaking Montparnasse of Ford Maddox Ford and Hemingway, and a perfectly dreadful little corner of a foreign field it is. They are the people who "[imagine] they know a thing when they know its name"—the artistic circles who, for the most part, perpetually circle art, whose only consistent contact with France is the habitual *fine à l'eau* in the same café.[1]

Lois Heidler "liked explaining, classifying, fitting the inhabitants (that is to say, of course, the Anglo-Saxon inhabitants) into their proper places in the scheme of things. The Beautiful Young Men, the Dazzlers, the Middle Westerners, the Down-and-Outs, the Freaks who never would do anything, the Freaks who just possibly might."[2] Mrs. Heidler (who addresses her husband as "Heidler") has pronouncements to make on everything—for example, on "sensitiveness, which she thought an unmitigated nuisance."[3] In her opinion, " 'Those sort of people don't do any good in the world.' 'Well, don't worry,' answered Marya. 'They're getting killed off slowly.' "[4]

What makes life possible for the Heidlers and their friends is taking themselves seriously. Among them, Marya is hopelessly disadvantaged by her superior sense of the ridiculous, by the ironic, tender view that enables her to understand her fate while making her incapable of preventing it. When Heidler falls temporarily in love with Marya, Lois teeters "on the brink of an abyss of sincerity."[5] Recoiling in time, she bullies the fallen Marya with a show of domestic virtue, and wins (although Heidler, hard, weak, and unhandsome, may be thought a doubtful prize).

Between them, the Heidlers reduce Marya to abject desperation. With their "mania for classification" they have tagged her a neurotic slut, and she finds herself trying, as it were, to live up to their expectations, importantly aware like a person in a dream.[6] Even as she notes Heidler's hypocrisy, his pomposity ("He looks exactly like a picture of Queen Victoria"), she grows more passionately dependent on his love.[7] Heidler, who has crudely seduced her (and the word is appropriate, for it is her loneliness that has been victimized, and her poverty) under the eyes of his wife, is shocked when Marya comments on Lois's big feet: "You've got to play the game," he says.[8] The Heidlers have made themselves invulnerable, but it is the strength of the officious and incurious. "It's all false, all second-hand," Marya longs to shout at them. "You say what you've read and what other people tell you. You think you're brave and sensible, but one flick of pain to yourself and you'd crumple up."[9] And coming away from the prison where she visits her husband, she reflects on the Heidlers and their confident circles: "How many of them could stick this?"[10]

Marya's pitiful husband, Stephan, completes the wreck on his release from prison—a wounded creature, nervously babbling of a new start in Argentina, whose small reserves of delicacy and unselfishness are inadequate to the crisis. A brief meeting between Stephan and the Heidlers contrasts the intuitive humanity of the ex-convict with the bumptious Person of Importance. Without one word of prompting from the author, one is made aware how preferable is the unappetizing Stephan, who still has the grace to be shy, to be anxious, to perceive. It is a moment of inauthenticity that can only be provided by life itself, or by great art.

"Misfortune," says La Fontaine, "is a kind of innocence."[11] Marya and Stephan are the innocents of this quartet. Each has been caught and humiliated by life, and each recognizes what it has done to them. The Heidlers are far too competent ever to acquire innocence in such a fashion: error and grief and absurdity have no place in their life-defeating formula for "success." And their destruction of Marya is in keeping with the elimination of all such unclassifiable threat from their program.

This is a short novel. The word "slight" cannot be used of a work in which so much talent is displayed. Miss Rhys tells her story with the miraculous spontaneity of all her writing, and in the tone of one who keeps calm while reporting a catastrophe. One must be glad that educated poverty has taken less annihilating forms since this book was written; otherwise, *Quartet* is vividly undated, directing our attention to paradoxes and pretensions that have become even more explicit in our present day. The reemergence of this fine novel at a moment when so much fiction tends to be bossy or calculating is in itself a heartening affirmation of what Jean Rhys has to say.

THE LASTING SICKNESS OF NAPLES

Review of Matilde Serao, *Il Ventre di Napoli*

This new edition of what had become a rare book is a literary by-product of the 1973 cholera outbreak at Naples. Matilde Serao's impassioned articles, published during the 1884 cholera epidemic in which almost 8,000 Neapolitans died, were first collected in a volume, with epilogue by the author, in 1905. In September 1973, within three weeks of the reappearance of cholera in the city, the book was reissued in the present paperback form, with an up-to-the-minute introduction by Gianni Infusino. The first printing sold out through individual orders before reaching the bookshops; the second was on the stands within days. And its new Neapolitan readers doubtless discovered in it the most knowledgeable and eloquent account of their city's past, present, and—one fears—future condition.

The book is, however, more—or other—than that. The parallel, an obvious one and frequently drawn, between Zola and Serao is here inevitable and valid. The literary meeting of outraged social conscience with a poetic vitality of image is not only rare but rarely complementary. In this case, an unerring literary instinct takes the work beyond the category of humanitarian appeals, where it would occupy a noble and foremost place, and into the range where all awareness is extended and which must therefore be called "art." The intensity of the narrative—doubtless subjected, in its time, to the indefatigable male adjective "shrill"—not only deepens urgency and poignancy but animates the whole with unquenchable life.

Matilde Serao was born before the Risorgimento and died after Mussolini came to power. Novelist, essayist, journalist, founder and editor of newspapers, she produced a large body of writings—including a number of novels, of which the singular *Il Paese di Cuccagna* is probably her masterpiece. *Il Ventre di Napoli* was the highly informed *cri de coeur* she addressed to a corrupt and indifferent officialdom, which—having in the 1880s, as in the 1970s, abandoned the city to privation and decrepitude—thundered rhetorically of illusory reforms when catastrophe struck. "*Bisogna sventrare Napoli*"—"Naples must be disemboweled"—was the official slogan from which Matilde Serao took her title. Her book does not deal with the effects of cholera but with the conditions in which the epidemic originated: the "belly of Naples," the bowels and entrails of the great city that to Leopardi was both "mistress of mortals"[1] and "Rat's nest"[2]; which Malaparte considered "a Pompeii that was never buried," not a town but a fragment of "the ancient pre-Christian world—which has survived intact on the surface of modern times."[3]

The book is history, also, and anthropology. A thousand arresting details of popular life and custom appear almost incidentally in its teeming canvas of survival. To say that the author writes feelingly of the torment of separate souls within the purgatory she exposes to us is to mock the fiery humanity of her work. While she condemns the empty sentimentalizing of extremity as "picturesque"—"*a diavolo la poesia e il dramma!*"—her own writing is a revelation in the authentically picturesque, in the truly poetic and dramatic.[4] In this brief book a society is rendered in all its strangeness, its wretchedness, its humiliations, its indomitable human graces. And the author marvels that civilization should have been preserved, mysteriously, in a people whom adversity and vice might have brutalized—but who, instead, love color and form and decoration, whose music is suffused with "invincible nostalgia," who have retained a sense of nature and of celebration, who, living in the dark, still love the light.[5]

Ninety years after publication, these chapters assail the reader with their application to present conditions—an ultimate vindication both foreseen and dreaded by the author. From Monte di Dio 10 Quartiere Vicaria, "the great sinful streets," as Clough called them,[6] the putrid alleyways, the very buildings themselves might today be named in almost identical context: the same squalor, the same decomposing glories—bedeviled now by cars, or blasted with the unredressed bombardments of 1943 but astonishingly, incontestably, the same. Unaltered, too, the evils of an administration, now hugely magnified in size, of whose monumental negligence it could already be demanded, almost a century ago: "To what purpose, then, are all these senior and junior employees, this immense bureaucratic machinery that costs us so dear?"[7]

The concluding third of the book, written twenty years after the epidemic, attacks as farce and fiasco the vaunted *risanamento* of Naples, when the boulevard of the Rettifilo was driven through a warren of ancient slums, carrying all before it—including the poor, for whom no provision was made in the new, expensive constructions that lined the route, and who reinterred themselves as best they could in the squalor, surviving undisturbed on every intersecting byway. For the symbolic Rettifilo itself—an avenue that no one could now regard as other than a prospect of unalleviated dreariness—Matilde Serao attempts a word of contemporary praise, but her perceptions are too much for her; and against that bleak new monotony, she sounds another warning, which will again go unheeded and will bring another sigh from modern readers who have helplessly watched the postwar inundation of Neapolitan jerry-building and the concomitant decay of an incomparable patrimony of art and antiquities:

> Alas, this is an evil common to so many other beautiful Italian cities where, side by side with ancient splendors and the supreme refinements of taste, modern architects have raised monuments to their own utter ignorance and total lack of aesthetic sensibility.[8]

This is a powerful book, and its author faced the bitter possibility that it might prove completely ineffectual. The weight of sheer official irresponsibility and venality ranged against her, compounded with the fatalism of the afflicted themselves, were understood by Matilde Serao as thoroughly as all the other elements of which she wrote. The reemergence of the book, however, and its phenomenal appositeness, testify to the endurance not only of affliction but of human indignation, also, and of potential remedy. Beyond the multiplicity of specific reforms she advocates, her "solution" (although she would not have employed so immature a term) remains fundamental:

> To eradicate material and moral corruption, to restore health and conscience to these poor people, to teach them how to live—they know how to die, as you have witnessed—to convince them that their existence matters to us, it is not enough to disembowel Naples; Naples must virtually be re-created.[9]

THE NEW NOVEL BY THE NEW NOBEL PRIZE WINNER

Review of Patrick White, *The Eye of the Storm*

Great literature is like moral leadership: everyone deplores the lack of it, but there is a tendency to prefer it from the safely dead. Contemporary writers who threaten to alter us with knowledge and extend us with pleasure and pain seem to pass through a period of ritual resistance from critics. Reviewers whimper that familiar ground is being reworked, that the latest books are not up to the early works (which they had inadvertently neglected to praise at the time), with the implication that this somehow invalidates the whole. During this interregnum, the writer's humanity is stigmatized as indulgence, his discernment as embitterment; he is getting soft, or hard, or nowhere. Until we submit, at last, to our own enlargement through the intention, revelation, and particularity of genius.

Of recent years Patrick White has been subjected to all these promising signs, as well as to merited and more agreeable forms of tribute from those who have admired this marvelous writer for decades. Imputing "inspiration" to novelists is as dangerous as discoursing on Nature with farmers: but each of White's novels has been blessed and quickened with a center of narrative power—a large meaning in which the author seeks to create our belief. Without at least some measure of this mysterious ignition, which is utterly distinct from "content," the most gently wrought book remains stationary and merely professional. White has always been able to command it in abundance: his novels, plays and stories are irradiations from related central themes in which the author participates no less intensely than his characters. All have on them the bloom of a bound humanity.

The Eye of the Storm is on the large scale of White's productions of the past twenty-five years: *The Aunt's Story*, the splendid *Voss*, *The Tree of Man*, *Riders in the Chariot*, *The Solid Mandala*, and *The Vivisector*. The matter in hand here is no less than existence: our brief incarnation in a human experience, our efforts to make a coherence of, or retreat from, the improbable combinations of flesh, feeling, vanity, virtue, and reason laid upon us like preposterous puzzles. Elizabeth Hunter is dying at a great age in her ornate house at Sydney. Once a surpassing beauty—who still occasionally has herself bedecked in lilac wig and rose brocade and, with sightless accuracy, fondles rubies and sapphires from her jewel-case—she is now a desiccated shred of former flesh, which nurses and domestics have for years contrived to oil and nourish. Turned on her side she is "like a deck chair upset by the wind" yet there is "some of the former mineral glitter in her almost extinct stare," and "rare coruscations occurred, in which . . . this fright of an idol became the goddess hidden inside of life, which you longed for, but hadn't yet dared embrace; of beauty such as you imagined, but had so far failed to grasp . . . and finally of death, which hadn't concerned you, except as something to be tidied away, till now you were faced with the vision of it."[1]

It is through Mrs. Hunter and her authority over the fact of being that her household and her son and daughter vicariously face death and, as a result, struggle to give consequence to life.

The realization that we are all living to a deadline cannot do much for Mrs. Hunter's aging children—the excruciated divorcee Dorothy and posturing Basil, a famous actor—who long since fled their mother's loveless clutches to nurture their grievances abroad and now return to "put her in a home"—that is, to deprive her of one in order to salvage their diminishing inheritance. Early sufferings have not ennobled this devious and fretful pair, whose stunted emotions are, even so, mainly engaged in panic-stricken efforts to withhold clemency, to ward off the unfathomable threat of grace. Reduced in her mother's presence to "a mere daughter," feeling "her nylons turn to lisle," Dorothy yet flails against her own "guilt, tenderness, desire, lost opportunities. She must never forget *Mother is an evil heartless old woman*."[2] To her children Elizabeth Hunter is "an enormously enlarged pulse dictating to the lesser, audible valves opening and closing in their own bodies."[3] Dorothy cannot accept her mother's mortality: "She was too cunning, cruel, to release you from your hatefulness by dying."[4] While Basil's quandary is to "make death convincing off the stage."[5] In all, a family tableau recalling Titian's *Pope Paul III with His Nephews*.

Waste of this kind, the squandering and perversion of qualities and capacities for whose exercise we are allowed so little time, has always preoccupied White, who exposes its pathos and irresolution without reducing its repugnance.

Elizabeth Hunter has lived a predatory life, and her power in part still derives from seeing through people rather than into them. Men and women have "looked up to her as somebody beautiful, brilliant—occasionally inspired"; and she has played dolls with them.[6] She herself is still "impressed by the emotional outburst it is in her power to cause," is still in awful possession of emotions she is "storing up against some possible cataclysm."[7] "Elizabeth Hunter never forgives: she lines you up for more of the same; which can amount to the same thing."[8] Yet she is almost without hypocrisy, is capable of self-knowledge and of a long remorse for the dead and gentle husband from whom she withheld love in life. Age had "forced her to realize she had experienced more than she thought she had at the time . . . that the splinters of a mind make a whole piece. Sometimes at night your thoughts glitter. . . . [You] know yourself to be a detail of the greater splintering."[9]

Years before, on an island holiday during which she appropriated her daughter's loutish, sunburned suitor ("she only half-wanted the Norwegian; he was peeling"), Elizabeth Hunter had been abandoned in the path and eye of a cyclone.[10] This is the thing itself, "it is the linesman testing for the highest pitch of awfulness the human spirit can endure."[11] She passes through destruction to become, in humble triumph, "a being, or more likely a flaw at the center of this jewel of light."[12] The exaltation of extremity cannot be sustained, but it marks her with knowledge: "Whatever is given you to live, you alone can live, and re-live, and re-live, till it is gasped out of you."[13]

Now, in a room that pungently smells of mortality, her handmaidens—the nurses de Santis (who is, literally, goodness itself), Manhood, and Badgery—tend Mrs. Hunter in shifting moods of love, revulsion, and loving revulsion, assisted by a tender lachrymose clown of a housekeeper. Mrs. Hunter can open the filial wound in each of them, but her dying body has come to be almost as their own, their only known fate, and the difficulty is to house their souls somehow there. Her old lawyer Wyburd uneasily fills the role of faithful retainer. Even the aging chaos of Dorothy and Basil, who appall him in their Regan-and-Goneril descents on his chambers, assails Wyburd's charitable memory "with the attributes he would have liked them to keep: grass-stained, scab-kneed, still a vision of potential good."[14] Wyburd is innocent, unrenowned. And the pretty, promiscuous nurse Flora Manhood wonders, "What makes people grow up decent? . . . It could be from not wanting anything enough."[15]

Basil and Dorothy dodge around their mother's intolerable presence as around the challenge of compassion—or greatness. They make a pilgrimage to the vast "still shamefaced landscape" of their rural childhood, Basil persuading himself that "at 'Kudjeri' perhaps he would rediscover the real thing—if there was enough of him left to fill so large a stage."[16] Their mother's death brings them scuttling out of the protective custody of a fascinated farmer and his homely wife and back into the carapace of self-pity. Still menaced by their better natures, they take the money and run.

Elizabeth Hunter has died at last—not through a withdrawal of will but by an assertion of it. She leaves some who, having nourished themselves on her essence, cannot live without her; and those who will give themselves to life because of her, passing into comprehension through the eye of the storm.

Echoing the book of Revelation, W. H. Auden decreed that novelists must " . . . among the Just / Be just, among the Filthy filthy too."[17] Patrick White extends this obligation to its larger dimension, discovering degrees of filth and justice in each existence, becoming his divergent characters with impassioned veracity rather than adapting them to his purpose. It is impossible that so ambitious a concept would be without any flaw of execution; but White's magnanimity, his logic, his poetry are not incompatible with the spirits he invokes by name—Shakespeare, Stendhal, Redon. Splinterings of James, of Joyce, of other writers male and female, make part of his own "greater splintering."[18] White's rich, distinctive language, now stately, now mercurial, always borne on the civilizing tide of irony, makes this big book as generous as it is demanding: every passage merits attention and gives satisfaction. In a creation intricate with the nerves and tissue of consciousness, women are predominant, rendered with a rigorous, luminous truth.

One seeks among debased superlatives for words that would convey the grandeur of *The Eye of the Storm* not in destitute slogans but in tribute to its high intellect, its fidelity to our victories and confusions, its beauty and heroic maturity. In *Voss* a character laments, "If I could but describe in simple words the immensity of simple knowledge."[19] It is knowledge, beyond all benefits, that this prodigiously gifted writer is conferring upon us.

The claim, continually made in American literary circles, that "here is where it's all happening" can cause the foreigner something of the surprise felt on learning that the World Series is a tournament in which no other nation participates. (Is there not, in any case, something parochial about the very insistence itself? As Jacques Barzun has said, self-assurance cannot be "shown.") Unless art is to be regarded as a competition, one can only wish "it" to be happening as extensively as possible. All Patrick White's books have been published here by the Viking Press but have had the minimum of attention in this land whose own fiction is increasingly oppressed by ethnocentricity of reference, range, content, and criticisms. White's reputation in the United States has been created in the most durable form: almost exclusively between himself and readers. (He has thus largely been spared "interpretation"—though this percussion is soon to break on him and with what clashing of symbols. Perhaps the reprieve has merely assisted him to speak out queer and clear.)

Novels or poems in translation—from Russian, French, Spanish, or Japanese—may more easily find a publisher in America than any new work of quality from Australia. A few Americans have perhaps heard, in the past, of Daisy Bates or Henry Handel Richardson, more recently of Christina Stead and A. D. Hope. Alan Moorehead is known (but not for his fiction), and Thea Astley has been published here. Incuriosity has otherwise been the rule.

W. J. Weatherby recently described in the *Times Literary Supplement* his fruitless pilgrimage through New York bookshops on the day the Nobel was announced for Patrick White. None of White's books was in stock. The grotesque riposte of the book business to this situation would of course have been, "We didn't know he was going to win the Nobel Prize."

The publishing and marketing of books is in a generally grievous state. However, in recent years it would always have been possible to find, in reputable London bookshops, not only a number of White's novels but also a selection of contemporary Australian writing—Hal Porter's heart-shaking *Watcher on the Cast-Iron Balcony*, for example, or a new novel by Elizabeth Harrower or Judah Waten. No American journal performs the service, provided in England by the *Times Literary Supplement*, of bringing new talents of the English-speaking world regularly to general attention. The Nobel citation itself proclaims that Australia has now been "introduced into literature"—as if literature were some august academy outside of which Australian writers had hitherto been practicing their art.[20]

As with all important novelists whose testimony implicates their native land, the fact that Patrick White is Australian is, from the literary standpoint, both essential and irrelevant. The hit-and-miss geography of the Nobel lottery, which has this time devolved on a master craftsman, will bring White more readers, but it is otherwise possibly of little consequence to a man immune to acclaim and obdurately remote from the distracting ritual of commercial caperings, pontification, and self-praise. Patrick White has donated his Nobel Prize money to the establishment of a fund for Australian writers, remarking (like his incorruptible Sister de Santis), "There is nothing I want." A man who is engaged in such an enterprise as his has no time to "want" anything—unless, perhaps, the well-being of other writers.

ORDINARY PEOPLE

Review of Barbara Pym, *Quartet in Autumn* and *Excellent Women*

Interest in the work of Barbara Pym was recently stimulated when several writers independently named her as Britain's most unjustly neglected living novelist. The two books now published in the United States—*Excellent Women*, first issued in England in 1952, and *Quartet in Autumn*, a new work—are in my opinion her very best so far. Her candid, penetrating humanity can be disconcerting, like a quiet, strong, perceiving presence in a busy room. Similarly, her wit forms an undercurrent of realization. Her distinctive style, while quite her own, belongs to an English tradition that in painting would include Gwen John, in literature Charlotte Mew: a stillness vibrant with a piercing sense of human frailty.

George Eliot, in her *Scenes of Clerical Life*, urges us "to see some of the poetry and the pathos, the tragedy and the comedy, lying in the experience of a human soul that looks out through dull grey eyes and that speaks in a voice of quite ordinary tones."[1] It is to this tragicomedy that Barbara Pym's talent is directed, and her *Quartet in Autumn* builds to a stronger pathos than her previous books. Four office colleagues—two male, two female—reach retirement age and face the slim pickings of pensioned obscurity. None has much in the way of inner or outer resources; and each has a fair measure of undistinguished eccentricity, developed throughout a doggedly parochial life. The extent to which change is intolerable to them dictates their diverse lonely fates. Among modern incongruities, their timid or rigid virtues are extinguished, along with an entire and helpless past, before our eyes.

Quartet in Autumn moves within a smaller compass than Muriel Spark's *Memento Mori*, which treats a similar theme; and Miss Pym is poignant, where Mrs. Spark is masterly. But this is fine, durable stuff, an originality that, however you approach it, gives back the truth.

Excellent Women is so entirely delightful that its tremor of pain takes the reader unaware. (As Miss Pym would say, "It was rather sad, really."[2]) The novel's narrator is a woman in her thirties, pious, comely, and kind, whose willingness merely to assist at other people's lives is taken for granted by her friends, and very nearly by herself. Here too an English dread of change acts as a brake on existence, let alone passion. (Transferred to a new room in a government office, one character laments: "Different pigeons come to the windows."[3]) The heroine's very worth practically ensures that she will be overlooked—a risk that Miss Pym herself has fearlessly run and triumphed over with the excellence of these two books.

TRANSLATING PROUST

I felt that this last sentence was merely phrase-making.
—Marcel Proust, *The Fugitive*

The ever engrossing question of rendering into English Marcel Proust's *A la recherche* still turns, irresistibly, on the adjusting or supplanting of Charles Scott Moncrieff's long dominant *Remembrance*, a work that having been the touchstone for generations of Proust's English-reading public continues—despite necessary amplifications, commendable reworkings, and persistent criticisms—to preside, a lion in the path.

"Reworking" is the word of the late Terence Kilmartin, in his prefatory note to the three-volume edition that, revised by him, incorporates in its final volume the translation of *Le temps retrouvé* by Andreas Mayor. These later translations had the benefit of the elucidated text, in the annotated Pléiade edition, of Proust's labyrinthine manuscript—dense, in its closing section, with the author's insertions and emendations as painfully indicated on his deathbed: matter that had seemed, to the eye of the layman, virtually indecipherable. Proust died in 1922; Scott Moncrieff in 1930. The "reworked" edition of *A la recherche*, revised by Kilmartin, is justly presented as "Translated by C. K. Scott Moncrieff and Terence Kilmartin," and retains its title *Remembrance of Things Past*. Working with close and sympathetic attention to Proust's words and intentions, Kilmartin made adjustments, for the most part necessary and pleasing, to Scott Moncrieff's version, paying tribute to that pioneering translation, which—as Kilmartin says in his prefatory note, has long been regarded "almost as a masterpiece in its own right."

Himself in ill health, Kilmartin—like Scott Moncrieff—carried his enterprise close to conclusion. That in itself marks him out among revisionists and critics of Scott Moncrieff. The road back from intended retranslations of part or all of the *Recherche* had come, over many years, to resemble those nineteenth-century paintings of the retreat from Moscow, in which somber marshals astride drooping horses lead an exhausted multitude through snowdrifts charged with the bodies of their fallen comrades. In the epic of retranslating Proust, considerations of time, health, finances, fatigue, and no doubt much else have contributed to withdrawals from the field. New millennial translations have as yet dealt with assigned portions, only, of the work. Whoever tackles Proust's novel is taking on the translation, from a most exigent original, of a million and a quarter words scrupulously assembled by one of the most prodigious and complex authors who ever lived. They are confronting, also, a nineteenth-century capacity for magnitude.

In 1853 Gustave Flaubert, seized with the creation of *Madame Bovary*, was already lamenting a literary decline, from the luminous power of the great masters into the troubled assiduity of contemporary writing: "We must pile up a mass of little pebbles to build our pyramids; theirs, a hundred times greater, were hewn in monoliths."[1]

The genius of magnitude nevertheless persisted, in its terminal phase, into the generation—to which both Proust and Scott Moncrieff belonged—that outlived the 1914–18 war: the Great War, with its everlasting debilitation of civilized conviction and sense of purpose. A reiterated commendation of Scott Moncrieff's approach to his task has logically touched on his close relation to the ambiance, atmosphere, and culture of the Proustian era. Proust's own concept of his immense endeavor had been visionary; as was the decision of his first English translator "to devote his life," in George Painter's words, "to the translation."[2]

A dozen years or more ago, during a particular irruption of criticisms of the Scott Moncrieff rendering, I set myself the game, on summer evenings, of comparing favorite passages of the *Recherche*—spreading the original, in the Pléiade volumes, alongside the Scott

Moncrieff, together with the "reworked" Kilmartin. One's lasting impression was one of admiration for both translators, and a renewed sense not only of Scott Moncrieff's achievement but of its importance as a precedent for every subsequent contender. The thing had been attempted, it had been done. It was incontrovertibly there—to be read, enjoyed, praised, patronized, carped at, disparaged. In the realm of translation, it is a colossus—daunting even to the most confident of its critics, since, if it is to be challenged, it cannot merely be "redone"; it must be conspicuously bettered.

These impressions brought to mind—with allowance for the great discrepancies of the analogy—remarks by the nineteenth-century historian François Guizot on his successive readings of Edward Gibbon's *Decline and Fall of the Roman Empire*:

> After a first rapid perusal, which allowed me to feel nothing but the interest of the narrative, always animated . . . and always perspicuous, I entered upon a minute examination of the details of which it is composed; and the opinion which I then formed was, I confess, singularly severe. . . . I allowed some time to elapse before I reviewed the whole. A second attentive and regular perusal of the entire work . . . showed me how much I had exaggerated the importance of the reproaches which Gibbon really deserved; I was struck with the same errors . . . but I had been far from doing adequate justice to the immensity of his researches, the variety of his knowledge. . . . I then felt that his book, in spite of its faults, will always be a noble work.[3]

Some such deference lingers with this reader toward the work of Scott Moncrieff in relation to the persistent, and sometimes derisive, criticisms to which it is subjected. Aside from essential inclusions of "new" material, and clearly justified modification, the quality of the huge task—accomplished in relatively few years and quite without the vaunted apparatus of modern electronic innovations (which, in fact, in artistic affairs, seem of little assistance when certain ineffable chips are down)—still commands wonder, still gives pleasure, still dispenses beauty. Kilmartin acknowledges his fundamental debt to his predecessor. It is unlikely that any full and future rendering into our language of this great novel will not build upon and appreciate Scott Moncrieff's achievement, by now historic—and moving, also, in its evocation of a past ability to embrace the impossible single-handed and carry it to term.

Readings of recent new translations of separate portions of the *Recherche* suggest that these most often fall below their best standard out of a wish to differ at all costs from Scott Moncrieff. Illustrations of that tendency appeared, some years past, in a lively article in the *New York Times Magazine*, where a group of prominent revisers tried their respective hands at retranslating Proust's celebrated opening sentence: "*Longtemps, je me suis couché de bonne heure*"—conveyed with faithful simplicity by Scott Moncrieff as "For a long time I used to go to bed early." This article was much discussed at the time on the New York literary scene, the verdict falling heavily—in my own experience, unanimously—in favor of Scott Moncrieff's unforced choice of words over the attempts, sometimes ingenious, sometimes desperate, merely to differ. Terence Kilmartin himself discreetly stuck with Scott Moncrieff's plain rendition.

That particular pitfall, familiar as it must be to experienced translators, inexorably lures them. Kilmartin himself is not immune, and in his "reworking" the temptation occasionally makes a significant appearance within more superficial flickerings. To my mind, it blights one of the most poignant exchanges between Proust's lovers—in the days when Albertine, ceasing to be the Prisoner, becomes the Fugitive.

On the eve of her secretly planned departure from Marcel's house, Albertine is invited by Marcel on a twilit drive out of Paris. In the carriage, in an atmosphere of dream, calm falls on their long-tormented relations. For the girl, aware that she is about to put an end to a situation grown intolerable, it is an episode of high sadness, which she invokes in her conclusion to a letter written to Marcel following their rupture:

> *Croyez que de mon côté je n'oublierai pas cette promenade deux fois crépusculaire (puisque la nuit venait et que nous allions nous quitter) et qu'elle ne s'effacera de mon esprit qu'avec la nuit complète.*

Scott Moncrieff translates this as follows:

> You may be sure that for my part I shall never forget that drive in a twofold twilight (since night was falling and we were about to part) and that it will be effaced from my memory only when the darkness is compete.[4]

Kilmartin's version:

> You may be sure that for my part I shall never forget that doubly crepuscular drive (since night was falling and we were about to part) and that it will be effaced from my memory only when darkness is complete.[5]

Kilmartin's impulse to supplant "a twofold twilight" produces an assault on the ear. "Crepuscular," written or spoken is unnatural in English usage, and distracting. Its sound, evocative in French, is ugly in our language—and more so, to my thinking, in its heavy-handed coupling with "doubly." Since this brief passage has importance in Proust's narrative (Marcel mean-spiritedly seizing on it as evidence of his having educated this ignorant girl) and recurs not only in the immediately following pages but much later in the story. Kilmartin is obliged to repeat the phrase, always with an unhappy effect. Scott Moncrieff's "twofold twilight" does not jar on the ear, and is at melancholy ease with its Proustian era. It may be criticized but not readily replaced.

Similarly, in the same brief letter, when Albertine urges caution on Marcel in dealing with car salesmen—"*Vous vous laisseriez monter le coup par ces gens*"—Kilmartin's "You would let yourself be taken for a ride" seems an unnecessary correction to Scott Moncrieff's version, that Marcel not let himself "be taken in." Kilmartin perhaps enjoyed the double entendre of the car salesmen and the ride, but the transatlantic note comes amiss from Albertine.

By which I suggest that Scott Moncrieff does not, as charged, always overstate the case, or add to the convulsions of an intricate story; and that his best plain words have been, at times, elaborately brought up to date.

When I, at sixteen and living in Hong Kong in the postwar years, was merely aware of the *Recherche*, with no idea of what was in store, I met, at a gathering, a handsome, reserved, and pleasant person, still young, who was introduced as Miss Scott Moncrieff. I already understood the name's literary significance. It was at once explained, in her presence, that she was—the niece, was it, or a cousin?—of the great translator. She was one of the few women to hold, then, a distinguished, and beneficent, position in the colony: and it occurred to me that she possibly wearied of her reflected glory. Later, the matter being discussed in her absence, I heard, for the first time: "Of course, the whole thing will have to be redone."

Not so easy as all that.

Here are two later versions of what will surely be a succession of versions. The first is by D. J. Enright, who revised Scott Moncrieff's and Terence Kilmartin's translations. The second is by Peter Collier, whose translation of *The Captive / The Fugitive* has been published by Penguin as part of Christopher Prendergast's team translation of Proust's novel.

> Dear friend, thank you for all the nice things you wrote to me. I am at your disposal for the countermanding of the Rolls, if you think that I can help in any way, as I am sure I can. You have only to let me know the name of the agents. You would let yourself be

> taken for a ride by these people who are only interested in selling, and what would you do with a motor-car, you who never stir out of the house? I am deeply touched that you have kept a happy memory of our last outing. You may be sure that for my part I shall never forget that drive in a double twilight (since night was falling and we were about to part) and that it will be effaced from my thoughts only when the darkness is complete. (Translated by D. J. Enright)[6]

> My dear friend, thank you for all your kind remarks. I am at your disposal and shall cancel the order for the Rolls if you think that I may be of assistance, and I do think it's likely. You have only to tell me the name of your agent. You would be liable to let yourself be taken in by these people who have only one thing in mind, which is to make a sale; and what would you do with a car, since you never go out? I am very touched that you should have kept such a nice memory of our last outing. Please believe that for my part I shall never forget this excursion and its twofold twilight (since night was falling and we were destined to part) and that it will never be erased from my mind until blackest night finally invades it. (Translated by Peter Collier)[7]

In different degree, these renderings strike me as suffering from what might be called translation fatigue—or more explicitly, version fatigue. To his impassioned (or, some would say, overwrought) rendition of *La Recherche*, Scott Moncrieff brought the irreducible advantage of precedence: he was breaking new ground. He would reveal Proust's masterpiece—as far as then possible, in its entirety—to the English-reading world for the first time, in the process disclosing and developing his own interpretative powers over word and mood. He had been at work on the translation some years before being formally, and rather awkwardly, confirmed as its English translator. Every subsequent translator of Proust into English has been necessarily and monumentally aware of this precursor, and of those who followed him. Flaws have been established and corrected, revisions have been attempted, vocabulary and syntax have been weighed for possible innovation and improvement. And consciousness of these handlings and fingerings may have elusively acted on, and dimmed, the freshness of impression that inspired Scott Moncrieff and excited his readers. Assiduity has edged out élan.

In the two later translations given above, the opening lines of the passage, dealing with the prosaic car, carry none of the tension inevitably existing between two lovers who, so recently parted in emotional exhaustion, are resuming tentative contact under a flag of truce. Awaiting word from Albertine, Marcel sees her handwriting with anxiety and expectation. In Scott Moncrieff's version, there is throughout this passage a tremor of context, ineffably conveyed: the reader is aware that Albertine's remarks about the car are prelude to—and pretext, merely, for—her reversion to the poignant twilit drive and her declaration of lasting love. We ourselves, as readers, open and begin her letter sensing that something more is to come. In the latter versions, however, the shift comes abruptly, so that concern for the car appears to be given equal weight with the girl's poetic invocation of loss and remembrance.

It is hard to see how this slackening can be avoided. In the case of Proust, translators, multiplying, will naturally give attention to the work of predecessors. And, in a greater context than that of this small passage, the trend of much contemporary writing turns away from distinction: flair, style, singularity are suspect as "rhetoric." The tendency, when not infused with violence, can be rigorously poker-faced, as if a regiment of Buster Keatons were policing our once-expressive language. Marcel himself, moved by the closing words of Albertine's letter, seeks to neutralize them as hyperbole, or traces in them his own civilizing influence over her youthful ignorance. However, the words will haunt him by their generosity, as does the dignity of this farewell.

Whatever his weaknesses, Scott Moncrieff did not forget that he was dealing with greatness—already then an embattled concept in literature. Many years earlier, Gustave Flaubert, inexorable but never abstract, had himself noted—in a letter of December 1852 to Louise Colet—a new pressure on writers to move away from their fertile eccentricities toward "the modern democratic idea of equality"; citing with disdain François Charles Fourier's observation that "great men won't be needed."[8] Distrust of stature, which leaves its reductive mark on much new writing, surely need not infect fresh renderings of past greatness.

INTRODUCTION TO GEOFFREY SCOTT'S *THE PORTRAIT OF ZÉLIDE*

Her early life evokes its eighteenth-century setting: a flat, fixed, ordered scene of Dutch manors and villages; of fields extending, almost level, to the cold sea. Overhead, a huge sky of changing light and measureless possibility. Her circumstances are cultivated, wealthy, well born; her immediate family affectionate, exemplary, conventional, confining. As she grows—as she enters "Society" and her twenties—singularities of temperament assert themselves. Unaffected, merry, flippant, confident, she possesses a measure of genius. To an exceptional degree, she is both formidable and enchanting, playful and obdurate. And "I must tell you, too, that Zélide herself is handsome," so James Boswell writes to her, using the name she has whimsically adopted; James Boswell, a captivated admirer and equivocal suitor.[1]

We hear nothing of female friendships. Her mother is dear to her, and indulgent. Her sister is resentful and a bore.

Zélide's wit and beauty, her prodigious intelligence are not without arrogance. For most of her life, however, pride will be countered by a disarming honesty of self-appraisal. Her Gallic rationality is similarly moderated by cordiality. Among her finest attributes is simplicity of conduct: springing from people disposed to take themselves seriously, she has little taste for self-solemnity. Free of national pride, she would, in later years, tell her dearest correspondent: "You and I, in the days of our friendship, were of no country."[2] With all the gaiety and ardor, some sweetness is lacking. It is, again, Boswell who reproaches her for according her goodwill indiscriminately: "Every one is at his ease with you. It is terrible."[3] He reminds her that a man—and even such an ambivalent suitor as himself—likes to enjoy primacy. For the same offense, the autocratic husband of Browning's "Last Duchess" had his wife put to death:

> She had a heart—how shall I say?—too soon made glad . . .
> She liked whate'er she looked on, and her looks went
>   everywhere . . .
> She smiled, no doubt, whene'er I passed her; but who passed
>   without
> Much the same smile?[4]

Yes, for love some particular tenderness is necessary. And the reader, hoping—naturally enough—for love, will have to follow Zélide through much curious experience before the unexpected requital.

Her qualities bring her renown and distinguished correspondents. Having seen her portrait, the king of Prussia advises her to "give up reading Fénelon."[5] She acknowledges that marriage, children, would be a solution—if commonplace—to her dichotomy of temperament, and to an increasingly motiveless life. Of herself she writes that she is secretly "somewhat sensuous."[6] Projects for wedding her fall through—not always through her own reluctance. In what she acknowledges to be an unattractive episode, she labors, vainly, to bring an unenthusiastic candidate to the altar—principally in order to draw closer to the man most worthy, and most appreciative, of her youthful powers. Constant d'Hermenches, the secret epistolary confidant whom she rarely saw, was himself married. In their letters at least, he and Zélide are intimates; in letters, they are lovers. During those years, he said, her radiance would have warmed the heart of a Laplander.

At thirty, she marries. In 1773, Isabella van Serooskerken van Tuyll becomes Madame de Charrière, choosing from among more notable suitors a prosaic, undemonstrative—but not unfeeling—pedant, the former tutor of her brothers. There is nothing inevitable in that willful decision, seemingly taken at random. There have been many encounters in her life, and many advantages; there have been travels, and much exposure to favorable chance; there has been such an unusual degree of independence that the choice must seem irrational. She cannot easily be claimed as a victim—of her sex, her era, her society. By now, she might be charged with a few victims of her own. She removes herself to her husband's modest château near Lausanne (where, although within easy distance of Ferney, she chooses not to meet Voltaire). The sky of possibilities, the open sea, the world of travel and discourse are now remote. Mountains and winter fogs enclose her; the lake is seldom stirred. The future is contracting.

Years pass. Merriment has no occasion. Intellect and rationality turn bleakly inward. She writes animated and interesting novels—whose autobiographical aspects alienate her neighbors and would the husband who patiently copies out her manuscripts. Her writings are talented and apposite; their purpose is not merely vengeful. Introducing a volume of her fiction that appeared in translation in 1926, Geoffrey Scott points out that her impulse "was to use all this tedium to good effect. . . . Her subject is human nature; she watches it in herself."[7] Writing, publishing, does not relieve her spirits. An obscure local love affair disappoints her, intensifying what has become despair.

Why does she stay? What not return to the world? Why not separate—or, as she might have done, divorce?

One summer, retreating to the mountains, she is visited by her grieved and excluded husband who, on return to his gloomy house, writes her a sad, fine letter that must have touched her but could not melt her heart—that heart, one thinks, by now more deeply frozen than any Laplander's. Years earlier, Boswell, dazzled as he was, had told her: "I fear Zélide is not to be found."[8] Not, certainly, by usual avenues.

Commentators have cautioned us not to insist unduly on the legendary analogy of her suspended life: the sequestered princess languishing for want of rightful awakening. All the same, the fable irresistibly comes to mind—in her case, enigmatically self-imposed. Nothing in all Zélide's unpredictable existence is more unlikely than the irruption of the brilliant boy, nearly thirty years her junior, who—first encountered during a rare visit to Paris—breaks through brambles and cold Swiss walls to bring her back to life: to bring her liveliness, love, and that intimacy of spirit, wit, and affection in which, perhaps, she had always believed but never trusted.

Benjamin Constant loved her and paid tribute to her to the end of his life. The ironic surname of this mercurial prodigy was, ultimately, valid in relation to her.

> We suited each other perfectly. But it was not long before we found ourselves in a relation of more real and essential intimacy. Madame de Charrière's outlook on life was so original and lively, her contempt for conventional prejudices so profound, her intellect so forceful, her superiority to average nature so vigorous and assured, that for me, a boy of twenty, as eccentric and scornful as herself, her company was a joy such as I had never yet known. I gave myself up to it, rapturously.[9]

Not since the correspondence with Hermenches—who, into the bargain, is Benjamin's uncle—has Zélide responded full-heartedly to another human soul. She has somehow maintained, through arid years, her best readiness of self and sensibility, her laughter, and the luminous generosity of her mind. One feels the release of it, her emancipation. She and Benjamin are happy, not only in their boundless affinity but, as lovers are, in one another's unstinted presence. Monsieur de Charrière himself enjoys Benjamin's company—partly, no doubt, because of the enlivening change wrought in his hitherto martyred wife; partly because of the reassuring discrepancy of age; and in part, perhaps, because Benjamin is fascinating, funny, and endearing.

Benjamin sits by her fire, by her desk, by her bed. We do not know how to define that reference to a "more real and essential intimacy."

Geoffrey Scott tells us that

> The hours went their round. And sometimes when the fire was steady or a single candle burned between them, he would watch the dark silhouette of her profile on the wall, and note the elusive beauty that even her shadow possessed.[10]

Thus, for eight years, Benjamin comes and goes. Her house, for him, represents serenity, stimulus, pleasure, and rigorous thought. They correspond, and his letters become love letters. Despite the convolutions of a libertine existence and divided personality, he sometimes dreams, preposterously, of eloping with her. Much about Benjamin Constant is preposterous—not excepting the preternatural comprehension in which his genius is rooted; and which, exercised on his own psychology and extraordinary life will, in his writings, secure his posterity.

Zélide not only fears the fated rupture but anxiously precipitates it: as ever, she is over-endowed with rational foresight and with a faculty for self-injury. Their parting, when it comes at last, is sublime—and perhaps, she feels, not inconclusive. When the subsequent dénouement arrives, however, she is astonished and appalled. Benjamin has moved away—but a few miles only: to Coppet, on the Lake of Geneva. Thereafter—and again, this time for years, and famously—he will linger there, in chaotic thrall to Zélide's volcanic neighbor, the brawny and brave Madame de Staël. Detaching himself from Enlightenment, he embraces Romanticism—and embraces, unequivocally, Germaine de Staël. His years with her, unenviably dramatic, will carry him into political and literary adventures, and turbulent *amours*. He will father a child, he will marry, divorce—and remarry the same wife. He will cut a figure both of folly and courage in the world of action. He will never lose his gift of observation and self-appraisal, and will turn it, uniquely, to literary account.

For Zélide, pride and a haughty resignation consume the remaining years. Her very submission resembles an act of iron will, further dispiriting her husband. ("It is recorded that for fifteen years she never took a walk outside the walls of his garden."[11]) She continues to write—but now these are dry writings that defend logic and reason through the convulsed years that conclude the eighteenth century. She performs acts of humanity and philanthropy, befriending solitary—and even outcast—young women, who find her admirable but . . . intimidating.

With the passage of years, she corresponds occasionally with Benjamin—who, struggling now in the toils of Madame de Staël, thinks tenderly of Zélide, and of the concord and delight of their shared years. Acknowledging the lack of synthesis in her being and her destiny, she tells him: "My life and my memories have no unity; my plan of life had none."[12]

As that life closes, she is regarded with awe by those few familiars who attend her. At her death, in 1805, she is sixty-five and has spent more than thirty years by the cold lake—perplexing, aloof, and disclosing only briefly her concealed fires, her great capacity for companionship and love. It was Francis Steegmuller who drew my attention to *The Portrait of Zélide*—seeing Geoffrey Scott's earlier work, *The Architecture of Humanism*, on my shelves, and referring to Zélide as a favorite work of his since youth. During the subsequent years of our marriage, *The Portrait of Zélide*, in different editions, was among books that accumulated in our rooms abroad—in France, in Italy. In every reading life, certain works are talismans, especially those read in early years. Francis had discovered *Zélide* soon after its first publication, when he was in his twenties, and he felt that it had influenced him toward the writing of biography, which would occupy the greater part of his working life.

He loved the book—for relating, with sympathetic intelligence, with integrity and beauty, the story of an engrossing life. He admired the close attention to established evidence and existing scholarship, and the truthful ease with which these were incorporated in the narrative, contributing to its authority and surprise. The period and its *mentalité*, and the culture of the Enlightenment, were already strong interests for him. With this work, Geoffrey Scott undoubtedly stimulated those affinities. Another theme that would develop and recur in Francis Steegmuller's writing is embodied in *The Portrait of Zélide*: that of the intelligent and gifted woman seeking to ripen and express her best powers, yet carrying within her an ideal of love unlikely to be realized. The Grande Mademoiselle, Isadora Duncan, Louise d'Épinay all became subjects for books by Francis. He considered and made preparatory studies for biographies—never completed—of Anna Comnena, the first woman historian; of Marie Mancini; and of Queen Christina. All those interests may owe, initially, something to his feeling for the story of *Zélide*.

When Scott's book appeared, in 1925, the name of Isabella van Tuyll was virtually unknown to the English-reading world. Despite much serious scholarship since then, and recent publication of her writings in France, Britain, and the United States, she is scarcely today a household word. Geoffrey Scott, who died in 1929 at the age of forty-five, was a forerunner and has occasionally been accorded by subsequent scholars, a condescension sometimes shown to precursors. Nonetheless, the literary intelligence and sensibility, the command of language with which Scott tells this story are qualities to be praised and envied. No one who reads *The Portrait of Zélide* will forget it. The book is unique, it is humane, it is delightful. It is art.

INTRODUCTION TO IRIS ORIGO'S *LEOPARDI: A STUDY IN SOLITUDE*

The modern highway that lies along Italy's Adriatic coast—overlooking, from a high ridge, a succession of old seaports, or elsewhere descending toward the shore—provides one of the beautiful excursions of the peninsula. An outward adventure of sky and sea is paired with the inland splendor of the Marche, an eastern region of Italy that, cultivated as Tuscany, spacious as Abruzzi—is less known to travelers than the Tyrrhenian west.

A visitor who, leaving the coastal road for a brief inland diversion, reaches Recanati will find a handsome hillside town with medieval and Renaissance indications of a long past importance: old squares and churches, grand houses, and an art gallery with masterworks by Lorenzo Lotto. From spring into autumn, the clusters of tourists—Italians and foreigners—who wander here are mostly day-visitors summering by the sea at Ancona or Pesaro, or pilgrims from the nearby shrine of Loreto who are on their way to Ravenna, or, possibly, to Venice. Most visitors will notice the lines of poetry long since posted, with excessive official zeal, on walls throughout the town. Some will call at Recanati's chief monument, Palazzo Leopardi, to ask the timetable for the guided tour there; and, on learning that they must wait, perhaps, as much as half an hour, may explain that their bus will soon be leaving. At which the custodian will gently smile, and wonder aloud why people come here in a hurry: here, of all places.

Palazzo Leopardi, slightly convex, stands above the incline of its piazza like a pale, bombé chest: a long, large, noble house of blond brick. Stately, also, is the staircase where the little tour assembles. The tone of the house, inside and out, is ivory. Sunlight enters. Nothing seems forbidding—rather, one is relieved to think that Giacomo Leopardi's excruciating youth was passed, at least, in a graceful setting upstairs, the three rooms of a prodigious library displace such casual reflections. We are no longer spectators, on our forgetful way from one notable site to another. The place re-creates in us its own silence: emotion over what was achieved here mingles with the pang for what was suffered.

Even if one has never seen a photograph, a postcard, of these upper rooms, the scene will seem familiar. Windows look out to the small building across the piazza, where once a girl worked at the loom and sang; here is the undulant descent to the distant sea; there, under immeasurable sky, soft hills precede the Apennines. Indoors, within the enfilade of rooms, the books are aligned in soft, old colors, coppery, rust, or faded brown, floor to ceiling; on a serious old table, the small, pale busts of poets.

For some sense of how this agreeable little city affected its most celebrated citizen nearly two centuries ago, one would need, through a solitary winter, to walk its deserted lanes in the failing light of Sunday afternoons. Nothing, however, can give us back the ageless isolation of such a town and its provincial populace in the first years of the nineteenth century: the monotonies of its customs, tasks, and toil, and of its few distractions; the pattern of its pieties, its lives and deaths. No ingenuity can restore to us the context of centuried silence and self-communing loneliness, the acuteness of impression and incident, in which an immense intelligence could, without assistance, inform itself and a great gift be obscurely nurtured.

In 1797, the year preceding Giacomo Leopardi's birth, an event affecting all Europe had shaken even little Recanati when Napoleon, following his triumphant irruption into Italy, had invaded the Papal States, in which Recanati was included. General Bonaparte himself had swept through Recanati with armed entourage—a spectacle that Giacomo's father, Count Monaldo, had not deigned to watch. The figure of Monaldo—weak, sententious, impulsive, intermittently touching, and contradictory enough to seem, at times, a cross between Polonius and Pulcinella—stands over Leopardi's youth as an apologetic shadow in thrall to Adelaide, the pitiless wife and mother, fanatical in her religiosity, monstrous in her exercise of power. Through Monaldo's ineptitude, the household, with its revenues and labyrinthine rooms, its servants and resident prelates, had passed early into her hands: husband and children lived in their palace as paupers, threadbare; dependent on her scant charity, fearful of her tyranny. Her own subjection was to bear a child each year. Of those sons and daughter, she gratefully lost several—her eldest son famously recording that when one of her children was ailing, "she did not pray to God that it should die, since religion forbids it, but she did in fact rejoice."[1]

The surviving children, unloved and uncaressed, knew their predicament. Companions in adversity, they shared affection among themselves; saw that their father would indulge them if he dared, and that their mother's severity was unnatural. Monaldo had chosen his bride from a neighboring noble family already intermarried with his own, and there were cousins to play and bicker with, and relatives who occasionally attempted—fruitlessly—to intercede on behalf of the Leopardi offspring. The second son, Carlo, and the first daughter, Paola, were, enduringly, Giacomo's dear companions and confidants. Solidarity was clandestine, within a huge solitude.

Monaldo defied his wife in one matter only: the acquisition of books. For that, the world is his debtor. Books came into the house from pushcarts, from provincial booksellers, from libraries of the defunct, from friends and bibliophiles: the classical authors, the poets, philosophers, and theologians; books on the natural sciences, on astronomy, on jurisprudence; lexicons and commentaries, erudite works in diverse languages and from all literate eras, together with some useless pedantry and sheer nonsense. A shy, tractable child, Giacomo sat to his studies among 25,000 volumes in the library that Monaldo had put at the disposal of the townsfolk. The Recanatesi made little use of it, but the child made it his own, delightedly, and in a way that would illuminate the world, likening his discoveries to the state of falling in love.

Mastering Latin, teaching himself Greek, Leopardi soon eclipsed his priestly tutors—who included an émigré abbé who taught him French. He taught himself English and German. From Monaldo, we learn that the boy conversed in Hebrew with a visiting group of learned Jews. Philology was his first intellectual passion, and the theme of his early monographs—an outpouring of erudition that Iris Origo justly calls "truly terrifying."[2]

Great sensibilities are born into exile. As he came to an understanding of his powers, and of the cruel seclusion of his existence at Recanati, Leopardi was not the first to feel homesickness for a setting he had never known—for the stimulus and sympathy of kindred spirits to whom art and thought, and the heart's affections, were supreme: a country that he had inhabited in books. The image of the youth bent over his worn papers—*le sudate carte*—in the freezing library, writing late into the night, brings to mind the mature Machiavelli in tormented exile near Florence, where, seated among his books at evening to write *The Prince*, he "entered the courts of the men of past times," posing questions as to the nature and motives of humanity. And those great minds of other centuries, "out of their magnanimity answer me. And for four hours I feel no tedium, I forget every anxiety: I no longer dread poverty, nor does death hold any terror for me. I immerse myself in them completely."[3]

So, too, the adolescent Leopardi, through the ancient masters, consoles his sadness and draws toward his vocation. Reading Homer and Virgil, "I tried to find a means of making mine, it if were at all possible, that divine beauty. . . . I begin to translate the best passages; and their beauties, thus examined and recollected, one by one, take their place within my mind, and enrich it, and bring me peace."[4]

The conjunction of spiritual and actual, transcendent in Leopardi's poetry, was within him from infancy. The solitary child counting the stars, peering from little Recanati into infinity, was subsumed into the boy reading Ariosto while youths in the street below sang of love. Sounds and songs of an outer world haunt his greatest poems, emphasizing his own exclusion. The coachman's young daughter, seated before her loom, sings in the window across the way, and the boy rises from his ancient books to watch and listen:

> I saw the clear sky, the sunlit streets, the orchards;
> Here, the far sea; and, there, the farther mountains.
> No mortal tongue can utter
> What then was in my soul.[5]

Paradox of art: in telling us that his feeling is inexpressible, the poet makes it felt, unforgettably.

Into adolescence he was sustained by a passion of expectation—that bright promise, which he would later call illusion, deception, "my mighty error, ever at my side."[6] In imagination he conjured from the world an eventual response worthy of his own ardent humanity and implicit in the glory of the universe: a response to be embodied in the tenderness of a woman yet unknown. Almost nothing of this would ever sweeten his existence; he would never know a requited or consummated love. The inward romances of boyhood—his idealization of a girl glimpsed at a window or greeted in the street, the charm of a fleeting visitor—were blighted by transience and early deaths. They were mocked at last, and terribly, by the revelation of his own affliction. In late adolescence, Leopardi woke from his dreams and infinite desires to the realization that he was deformed. A curvature of the spine—probably scoliosis, presumably aggravated by the years of sedentary study that had also damaged his sight—would never leave him. Already misshapen, he would become a hunchback. Lest he should delude himself, the urchins of Recanati flung snowballs and pebbles, jeering at his frailty. In the celebrations of a feast day, a girl turns from him, oblivious, to smile on other admirers. Nature had marked him out for sorrow:

> I deny all hope to you, she said—yes, even hope.
> And your eyes shall not be bright for any cause,
> Except with weeping.[7]

Desolation "hurt him into poetry."[8] When he was nineteen, Leopardi's translations from Virgil drew the attention of learned men in Italy. A year later, his *Canzoni*, exalting Italy's past and inciting his contemporaries to restore her independence, fired the insurgent youth of his country, restive under foreign dominion. The greatest poems, the *Canti* of longing and mortality, were in gestation; but the "political" themes of the *Canzoni* are themselves charged with intimate fellow-feeling and with a compassionate fatalism for helpless lives eternally mauled by power and persecutions:

> Dear souls, in as much as your tragedy is infinite,
> Be at peace. And may this comfort you—
> That comfort none shall have
> In this or future ages.[9]

All the inner life of the years at Recanati is now at the service of his later experience and his genius. Renown, he thinks—for he is beginning to be noticed—may compensate a little for lack of love. It never does. In the great world, there may be women who, disregarding his infirmities, will love him for his qualities. He never finds them. To his parents' horror, and, in part, to his own regret, religious faith deserts him. Losses and deprivations, and the disappointment of unattainable dreams, are the stern stuff from which Leopardi will now fabricate beauty. He knows that even if he is to carry his birthplace with him all his life, as a burden and a precious lode, he must leave Recanati.

When Leopardi arrived in Rome in 1822, he had fifteen years to live. Subsequently, in Florence and Pisa, Bologna and Milan, he would meet with kindness and esteem; and, in spite of physical and mental suffering, take some pleasure in daily life. In Rome, too, he would be valued by some discerning minds. Rome, however, was the first city he knew outside his native habitat, and the goal in which he had placed his hopes. He reached it in November, over his parents' bitter opposition, and spent the winter there. Rome, then, was active not only with intellectual, clerical, and scholarly life but also as a gathering place for gifted foreigners—artists and antiquarians, poets and novelists who arrived with eager curiosity and marveled at what they found. We might have imagined the young Leopardi exclaiming, as the classicist Winckelmann had said of all Italy: "God owed me Rome, for I had suffered so much in my youth";[10] or with Goethe, "I, too, am in Arcadia."[11] Instead, our own hopes that have gone with him to Rome are baffled by his obdurate disappointment. And we begin to understand that for Leopardi there will be no rescue, and to sense the fateful course of his life.

Ill and ill-clad, penniless, naturally shy, and miserably sensitive of his affliction, the poet felt to the full the anonymity of city life. The grand, busy spaces and great monuments of Rome recalled to him not merely his own exclusion but the contrast of power and magnificence with what he held most dear: the innermost humanity of the singular spirit. Women, from whom, in that larger world, he had hoped for understanding, passed him with indifference or aversion. At the tables of learned men, he found vanity, rivalry, self-assertion, and obsession with theory and explication. Even while we wonder at Leopardi's aloofness from the magic of his surroundings, much of this will strike a chord in the modern city-dweller, for whom such conditions are today grossly magnified. He perceived the trend toward volume, velocity, novelty, abstraction; the blunting of insight and intuition, the incapacity for wholeness, the denial of mortality: an infatuation with system that would generate its new chaos. He saw culture without simplicity or profundity—much less that rare convergence of the two, which was his own surpassing distinction. It is Leopardi's ability to weigh these losses within infirmity, and yet as private pain, that makes his voice unique.

W. H. Auden, writing of Cavafy, observes that such a gift leaves "nothing for a critic to say, for criticism can only make comparisons. A unique tone of voice cannot be described."[12] Leopardi, by contrast, appears at first accessible to comparison with a number of great poets: with Poliziano, or with his own fellow Romantics, or above all, with Keats; or with the inexorable clarity of Thomas Hardy. Leopardi's mighty, uncompromising poem *La Ginestra*—"The Flower of the Broom"—which, set on Vesuvius, contrasts Nature's infinite indifference and tenacity with the ephemeral works and aspirations of humankind, offers curious parallels, also, with *A las Ruinas de Itálica*, a work by the seventeenth-century Spanish poet Rodrigo Caro.[13] While themes and sentiments will frequently coincide in literature, however, genius rarely strikes the same note or the same lightning. Leopardi, to my mind, is utterly and instantly distinctive. My own connection with him was formed when I was seventeen: standing in a bookshop ten thousand miles from Recanati, I opened a blue volume of new translations by John Heath-Stubbs. A little later, the revelation of Leopardi's life was supplied by the present work: Iris Origo's admirable and deeply felt biography.

Leopardi spent his last years at Naples, a city that had never lost its millennial roots in Greek civilization and which even yet remains an arcane theater to its familiars; where, far from shunning his deformity, passers-by might touch him for luck, for he had been honored by the attention of the gods. As, indeed, he had. He had been drawn to Naples by the affection of Antonio Ranieri, the younger friend who became his companion. The Neapolitan Ranieri shared Leopardi's penurious existence, cared for the captious invalid in his decline, and solaced his final sufferings. It was he who, in a time of plague, retrieved Leopardi's body from interment in a common grave. To the unsatisfactory figure of Ranieri, much is owed—one wishes it were less. But Ranieri alone, in

Leopardi's life, provided the loyalty and attachment of which the poet had once so differently dreamed.

Leopardi's grave—cared for, now, and visitable—lies on a slope near the Naples shore, in a small park that shelters one other memorial, a Roman tumulus long claimed, and still venerated, as Virgil's tomb. It is marked by an austere column of pale stone, bearing emblems of wisdom and immortality. The end of Leopardi's impassioned life is prefigured in one of his last poems, "The Setting of the Moon," which includes the line "Desire still alight, and hope extinguished."[14]

WILLIAM MAXWELL

In his eighties, William Maxwell told me, "I love being old." By then, Bill Maxwell had recurrent and sometimes serious bodily infirmities. His mind and spirit were perhaps at their ripest power and would remain so until his death, ten years later. Those years were blessed by his long and luminous marriage, by his love for his daughters, and by the birth of the grandson who so resembles him. Bill had long since been delivered from the burden of what had been to him, in earlier years, an incapacitating sensibility: the "difficulty of being" no longer held terrors;[1] "Fear no more the heat of the sun."[2] His advancing age was as yet no hindrance to new work, and was enriched by the close affection of friends and by the homage to his art and his character that, having come rather late in his writing life, was now overwhelming and worldwide.

William Maxwell's life, considered in outline, might seem quite divided. The childhood he would look back on as enchanted in its security—of place and family life, and through his mother's tender love—had been sundered by excruciating loss and loneliness. His mother's early death haunted Maxwell's life and work, and played its powerful part in the making of a writer. He understood this very well: few men have understood themselves as deeply.

The transformation came through his chance meeting with Emily Noyes, and the development of their great, reciprocated love. The ground, however, had been in some ways prepared. There had already been a measure of rescue by language and literature, and by the discovery and exercise of talent: the painful rescue, as it often is, through self-expression, intelligence, imagination. Maxwell was not drawn to intellectualism. His gift lay in acute humane perception. His response to existence derived from vulnerability and from intensity of observation.

I don't seek here to "explain," only to give impressions from an unclouded friendship of forty years. Bill Maxwell took my first writing from the slush pile of the *New Yorker* and published it. He then took the trouble to get in touch with me and asked me to come and see him at the magazine. His encouragement, his genius, and his generosity transformed my own experience—as they did the lives of other writers. When I met Francis Steegmuller, who became my husband, we found an immediate, talismanic bond in the discovery of shared friendship with the Maxwells. Francis had known Bill since their youth at the infant *New Yorker*.

The human encounter came always fresh to Maxwell. Singularity was intrinsic to his own nature and to his sense of other lives. He knew the world deeply, yet remained accessible to it, detached from the contemporary trend toward exposition and pronouncement. That he kept faith with the wound of his early knowledge helped him, I think, to become a happy man.

Alec Wilkinson has splendidly written that Maxwell, in conversation, considered the effect of his words on the person whom he addressed. This does not, I feel, suggest that Bill's responses were always acquiescent or uncritical—although indeed he was an embodiment of the sympathy and tolerance apparent in his very being. But disagreement was, with him, a reasoned matter: he was free of mere self-assertion. His views were large, but firm. Inauthenticity, calculation, and underhandedness drew his testy dismissal. He would not praise writing that he found spurious, no matter how expertly presented.

I believe that Bill would have felt the validity of Graham Greene's remark that the novelist conserves a splinter of ice in the heart.[3] He had the writer's need to defend the secret writing mind, where objectivity and syllables must alike be nurtured and weighed, and the deeper, unshared self explored and plundered for treasure.

The rescue that came to him in the middle of his life was favored also by the climate of the *New Yorker*, where Bill worked for forty years—with Harold Ross, the first editor, and at length with William Shawn. Both Ross and Shawn, in contrasting ways, were oddballs and had a feeling for the talents of fellow oddballs. Ross had a reputation for cryptic humor and a brash attitude for creativity. Shawn, unprecedented and unreproducible, remains an irreducible figure in the cultural story of New York or any other city. In late years, Maxwell had his differences with Shawn. But the decades during which they worked closely and cordially together were a period of rich literary achievement that, I imagine, no prominent magazine will ever enjoy again. To have been associated with the *New Yorker* during that period was revelatory, fascinating, and fun. Maxwell brought his generosity of spirit to the work of others. His feeling for one's work was never, in my experience, intrusive. He respected the creative intention. He loved fiction and loved the stories of our lives. His relations, of trust and tact, with authors are finely attested in his published correspondence with Frank O'Connor.

Maxwell paid tribute, in conversation and interviews, to another phase of his emergence from the griefs of his early years, saying that the psychoanalyst Theodor Reik had given him "a life." Two of Bill's comments on Reik's interventions seem at variance with Maxwell's temperament, although he relates them in a favorable sense. Reik felt that Maxwell should more actively seek recognition in his writing career, should be more ambitious for winning prizes. Yet it is precisely Bill's characteristic restraint in these matters that, viewed from the perspective of his long life, appears to have deepened the wide recognition that eventually came to him and, in retrospect, even seems to have mysteriously compelled it. Maxwell's instinct in this was appropriate and true. Bill also cites, again seemingly with approval, Reik's prohibition: "No remorse, no remorse." In both these correctives, it is hard to recognize Maxwell, and it seems possible that the analyst was seeking to reverse an excess of diffidence or self-accusation. A remorseless person is not an attractive phenomenon. Through responsibility and regret we come to know ourselves, and Maxwell's personality and writings attest to these qualities in their consideration for the sensibilities of others. Bill told me that he had, in latter middle age, written to each of several persons whom he thought he had wronged in earlier years: an exercise in apology and—one would have thought—remorse. On this theme, one thinks of Yeats:

> Things said or done long years ago,
> Or things I did not do or say
> . . .
> Weigh me down, and not a day
> But something is recalled,
> My conscience or my vanity appalled.[4]

In his last extraordinary year of life, while Emily Maxwell was slowly dying with a grace, a philosophy, and, I would say, a beauty that remains indescribable, Bill Maxwell reread *War and Peace*. His solace and pleasure in the book were an event in those rooms. He said, "It is so comforting." We rejoiced together over certain scenes, not "discussing" or dissecting them but paying, simply, the tribute of our delight. He would speak of these episodes shedding his silent tears—not in grief but for the grandeur of common humanity. Bill was steadily eating less, and when the book became too heavy for him to hold, a friend—Annabel Davis-Goff—came each afternoon and read it for him.

Five days before Emmy's death, the Maxwells, in wheelchairs, went to the Chardin exhibition at the Metropolitan Museum. Two days before Emmy's death, and ten days before his own, Bill finished reading Tolstoy's novel. The events encompassed in that last month of their lives, the tenderness quietly exchanged among the friends who visited them were entirely consonant with the qualities of that departing pair: unforgettable, unforgotten.

Bill Maxwell said that he did not fear death but that he would miss reading novels. In his own novel *The Château*, the American protagonist walking in autumnal light through streets and public gardens: "'*I cannot leave!*' he cried out silently to the old buildings and the brightness in the air, to the yellow leaves on the trees. '*I cannot bear that all this will be here and I will not be.*'"[5]

PART 3

Public Themes

THE PATRON SAINT OF THE UN IS PONTIUS PILATE

The UN Secretariat marked the twenty-fifth anniversary of the Universal Declaration of Human Rights by a last-minute withdrawal of promised facilities for Amnesty International's conference against torture—for fear of offending governments engaged in that activity from Saigon to Santiago.[1]

There was no outcry from accredited internationalists. Secretary-General Waldheim declined to condemn torture in his commemorative address, and opposition to torture was interred in yet another United Nations resolution of predetermined uselessness. Of thousands of documented cases of persecution submitted by Amnesty to the UN, not one has ever been forwarded for action to the United Nations Commission on Human Rights.

Soviet dissidents have marked Human Rights Day with placards in Red Square and hunger strikes in prison. Their appeals to the secretary-general receive no acknowledgment, nor does Mr. Waldheim utter one word for Aleksandr I. Solzhenitsyn, or for Andrei D. Sakharov or Roy A. Medvedev, whose supreme moral examples may cost their lives. The secretary-general has "no authority" to respond to Austria's appeal for United Nations assistance with emigrating Soviet Jews.[2]

A senior UN official informs a deeply demoralized staff that "the United Nations deals in the realm of what is possible, not of what is right or wrong." Extolling the United Nations' "moral impact,"[3] the secretary-general calls on history to bear witness—as it will—that he took no position on Vietnam.

There is no such thing as official cowardice. All cowardice—like all true courage—is personal.

I know of no setting where idealism is ridiculed as at the UN, where "realism" and "the possible" are so often equated with conformity and fearfulness, where the personal initiative and public engagement from which all human advancement proceeds are less nurtured or esteemed, no place more remote from acts of intellectual and moral courage, more incapable of distinguishing between discretion and poltroonery. The patron saint of the UN is Pontius Pilate.

With lip service to other values, UN authorities conspired with the State Department in the 1940s and with McCarthyism in the 1950s, and ignored the antiwar movement of the sixties.

In the 1970s, UN leaders preside over a system incapacitated by gross mismanagement, malpractice, discrimination, and illicit government pressures. Performance and principle flagrantly diverge—as when, amid UN proclamations for women's rights, an internal study warns that "nothing can explain away the massive facts" of virulent UN discrimination against its own female staff.[4] I recently spoke at the UN at the invitation of thoughtful senior officers who, like many of their colleagues, have appealed in vain to authority against the corruption and wasteful chaos in which opportunity is daily cast away.

No amount of such evidence here will arouse UN leadership—except against myself. Nor, far more significantly, will it bring inquiry from professional UN well-wishers, the elders among whom are sometimes as eager as the UN officialdom to deride idealism and deny the public any UN role beyond financing.

The UN is not a private philanthropic enterprise staffed by volunteers, but a world institution where tens of billions in public money have been disbursed by highly paid administrators. A full-scale citizens investigation, of the Nader type, is imperative if, from this shambles, the concept of world authority is to be reconstituted in contemporary, responsive forms.

"The great hopes of all mankind"—which, as Mr. Solzhenitsyn reminds us, were betrayed at the United Nations' birth[5]—not only envisioned publicly an accountable UN instrument but also, necessarily, the vigilance of international jurists, humanists, the responsible journalists acting as agents of stimulus and exposure in order to counter adverse national government pressures. Greatly to the relief of governments, this high potential was quickly broken on a wheel of seminars, social events, academicism, and Establishment contacts totally removed from perspective and actualities; and diverted to indulging, instead of denouncing, an institution where nationalism reigns supreme—just as earlier internationalists, ignoring the urgings of John Maynard Keynes and H. G. Wells, were seduced into promoting the tragic sham of the League of Nations to its hideous conclusion.

While the archaic pattern of nationalism is convulsed in unprecedented physical and social transformations, global power has passed, undisciplined, to technology and the multinational corporations.

It is ludicrous to suggest that the present important UN, conclusively reduced to abject servility in its current Middle East "role," could regulate such forces. Only direct, unsparing public pressure, soon to be released by drastic events and expressed by an indignant new generation, can now initiate human systems as global as our emergencies. There is no reason, however, why the present travesty of the United Nations—unable even to denounce torturers, or praise the brave—should meantime continue unchallenged, unscrutinized, and unreformed.

"GULAG" AND THE MEN OF PEACE

Last winter Aleksandr Solzhenitsyn's *The Gulag Archipelago* was published in Paris in Russian, and appeared in the bookshops of the West—including two Swiss bookshops long licensed to sell on United Nations premises in the Palais des Nations at Geneva. The director-general of the UN Geneva office, clandestinely acting at the instigation of the Soviet government, promptly caused the book to be removed from the Palais shelves, along with Solzhenitsyn's other works. Shortly thereafter, one of the bookshops—Messrs. Payot—closed. At the surviving establishment, that of Naville & Co., the subsequent English and French editions of *The Gulag Archipelago* likewise briefly surfaced and submerged.

Under the UN Charter, the organization's international staff are sworn not to "seek or receive instructions from any government";[1] under the Universal Declaration of Human Rights they are bound to uphold the free circulation of ideas and information "through any media and regardless of frontiers."[2]

United Nations censorship of Solzhenitsyn's works aroused comment in the European press, which reported a courageous protest by 250 of the several thousand UN employees at Geneva. On July 4, during a press conference at Geneva conducted jointly by the UN secretary-general Kurt Waldheim, and his subordinate, Vittorio Winspeare-Guicciardi, director-general of the Geneva office, the latter revealed that UN "guidance" had been at work in the Palais bookshops over many years.

Speaking of his "responsibility" and even "duty to inform Payot orally and confidentially" of the displeasure felt by "certain delegates" at finding Solzhenitsyn's book displayed, Mr. Winspeare-Guicciardi ignored the fact that his duty and responsibility are explicitly to the contrary. The bookshops too had "their duty," in his view, to avoid "*publications à caractère outrageant pour un Etat Membre*." The furtive means by which pressure was applied to the bookshops—"my, should I say, discreet way of dealing with the matter"—was emphasized; and Mr. Winspeare-Guiccardi concluded, "These are the facts of February."[3]

Mr. Waldheim himself introduced his elucidation with an affirmation of adherence to "the long-standing principle of freedom of information."[4] Indeed, in 1972, when Solzhenitsyn in his Nobel address condemned the UN as "immoral" for betraying its obligations under the Universal Declaration of Human Rights, Mr. Waldheim had stated that he "would be the first to welcome any initiative" toward honoring that covenant.[5]

"*Doublethink*," wrote George Orwell, "means the power of holding two contradictory beliefs in one's mind simultaneously, and accepting both of them."[6]

There were, it will be recalled, other "facts of February." In that month Aleksandr Solzhenitsyn prepared, in unexampled challenge to the forces of organized inhumanity, to lay down his life for those causes to which the UN is nominally dedicated. His hostages to fortune were his wife and children. The immediate issue was the publication outside Russia of his *The Gulag Archipelago*, the ultimate issue those liberties enumerated in the Universal Declaration of Human Rights. Unfortified in his long struggle by any word from UN sources, Solzhenitsyn, in his own words, "was upheld by the unseen, unheard thread of popular sympathy . . . and the world brotherhood of writers."[7] On the afternoon of February 12, Solzhenitsyn was dragged from his home by the Soviet police, and on February 13, deported into permanent exile.

During these great and terrible events, UN leaders could find no better occupation than to arrange, by stealth, for removal of Solzhenitsyn's works from international territory.

The Gulag Archipelago is a firsthand account of the most prolonged and extensive violation of human rights in recorded history—furnishing the very substance with which the UN was created to deal, and with which it has pitilessly declined to concern itself. Had a comparable chronicle been smuggled to the world from Dachau in the 1930s, it would—being offensive to the fascist membership of the League of Nations—have met an identical reception at the Palais. (The secretary-general of the League, Sir Eric Drummond, who permitted his Italian staff to wear the fascist emblem, had similar antennae for the "*outrageant.*") Mr. Waldheim himself, who served as an officer in Hitler's army on the Russian front described in *The Gulag Archipelago*, should be no stranger to the context in which such evils occur.

The secretary-general has received protests from PEN, and myself; I should be glad to hear of others. The world has heard nothing from those agencies and publications, those jurists, academics, and public persons who have attached themselves to an institution rather than to a set of principles, nor from the huge, and hugely timid, preponderance of UN officials. For failing to denounce inhumanities, Solzhenitsyn reminds us, "every man has at hand a dozen glib little reasons."[8]

Thus the embargo imposed upon Solzhenitsyn's writings in his native land has been, with exquisitely indicative irony, reproduced on the international territory of the UN—the organization charged with defending the free expression for which Solzhenitsyn was ready to give his life. Is there a writer among us who would not, in these circumstances, prefer to be considered "*outrageant*" at the UN? We may assume that Confucius long since vanished from the Palais bookshop; and that Aristophanes was, until last month, as unwelcome there as in his homeland. Some "discreet way" will perhaps be found of eliminating books on Watergate or ITT. Naville & Co. may eventually wish to proceed into exile from UN territory and seek literary asylum in the free world.

* * *

Editorial comment: In a letter to the editor of the *New York Times*, published October 6, 1974, the UN spokesman André Lewin responded to what he called Shirley Hazzard's accusation that Secretary-General Waldheim had "censored" Solzhenitsyn "by prohibiting the sale of his books in the bookshop located at UN European headquarters in Geneva," insisting that "there is no ban or censorship whatsoever in the bookshop of the United Nations" and that Solzhenitsyn's books "are sold there."

Hazzard was granted a response to Lewin, also published October 6, 1974:

> I do not accuse the United Nations of censoring Aleksandr Solzhenitsyn's works at bookshops under its influence: I state it as an incontrovertible fact.
>
> Readers of Mr. Lewin's deceitful and injudicious letter may obtain United Nations press release SG/SM/2033 of July 5 giving the UN's own account of its policy of censorship and the clandestine UN interventions at Geneva that resulted in commercial book sellers on international territory "referring their customer to shops in town" for purchase of works by Solzhenitsyn.
>
> Exclusion of Solzhenitsyn's works from UN premises, at UN and Soviet instigation, began last winter and was maintained—as the unfortunate Mr. Lewin reveals with his reference to "settling the matter"—into the summer. Mr. Waldheim's farcical invocation of the principle of freedom of information was in fact made during this ban and, as Mr. Jerzy Kosinski pointed out in his PEN protest of August 1, with no indication of lifting it. All this was reflected with perfect accuracy in my "Guest Word" of August 25.[9]
>
> On August 28, three days after publication of my article, the director of the UN Geneva office informed Mr. Kosinski, in a letter of two sentences, that Solzhenitsyn's works had at last made their reappearance on UN premises.

Mr. Lewin's shameless misrepresentation intensifies the ominous light shed by these events. What matters is not, of course, that Solzhenitsyn's work has finally been admitted to UN premises as a result of cumulative public pressure, but that it was ever removed and for months proscribed by our custodians of free expression. Mr. Waldheim and his subordinates have now compounded their dishonor with a mendacious, blustering attempt to conceal it.

Mr. Lewin has most unwisely called my statements "unfounded." I am more than ready to substantiate these matters at law. That my own role here is simply to illuminate abuses of public trust does not mean I will tolerate libels.

In my article of August 25, I conjectured that Confucius would find himself among the victims of UN servility to totalitarian decrees. I now learn that a quotation from Confucius was removed from the walls of the UN headquarters in New York on September 17, on instructions from the government of China[10]—and no doubt in pursuance of Mr. Waldheim's concept of "the long-standing principle of freedom of information."

THE UNITED NATIONS

Where Governments Go to Church

In that rarest of official documents, a moving statement, the League of Nations High Commissioner for Refugees performed, in 1935, that rarest of diplomatic acts: a resignation on principle. Denouncing the league's evasion of the desperate plight of German Jewry and appealing for prevention of "an even more terrible human calamity," James McDonald told the league: "I cannot remain silent. . . . When domestic policies threaten the demoralization and exile of hundreds of thousands of human beings, considerations of diplomatic corrections must yield to those of common humanity."[1]

A person holding such views could no more remain at the league than, subsequently, at the UN. It was the very function of the league to maintain silence on governmental crimes against humanity; and of its permanent officials to rationalize this silence as necessary to some never analyzed but paramount objective. The league was as unlikely to address itself to Nazism as was the UN, later, even to debate the destruction of Southeast Asia.

Current Third World activism at the UN is merely shedding intensified light on this fundamentally national nature of the UN enterprise. The UNESCO action against Israel, for example,[2] is new only in the measure of public indignation it has attracted: analogous violations have long taken place within the UN system, and the UNESCO episode in fact dramatically exemplifies a general condition.

Why governments should twice in our century have constructed an elaborate and costly "international" enterprise for the apparent purpose of incapacitation and perverting it—deliberately creating, as John Maynard Keynes observed of the League of Nations in 1919, "an unequalled instrument for obstruction and delay"—becomes clearer with the accelerating globalism against which it is paradoxically set.[3] Both international organizations were a channeling off, by national and economic power, not only of corrective reactions by populations to successive world wars but of growing efforts to adapt public institutions to the irresistibly planetary nature of the age.

As each world war drew to its close, it stood to reason that a responsible segment of enfranchised society would challenge governmental conduct of international relations; and that this challenge, heightened by nuclear terror, would in turn be recognized by governments, be nominally appeased, and rendered harmless or even profitable to national objectives.

To thwart a large public movement by leading its few spokesmen to an empty UN and locking them in must have seemed to our governing forces a surprisingly easy task; and the facility with which it has been twice accomplished remains a major puzzle of contemporary affairs. On both occasions national interests succeeded in diverting the energies of internationalists to the maintenance of institutions where nationalism reigns supreme, short-circuiting an important articulation of public opinion and exposure.

In the UN, as in the league, a perfect paradox was created: an institution that would proclaim standards only to undermine them; that would profess beneficence while condoning—actively or by silence, or through inconclusive debate—every form of barbarism. These apostasies were enclosed in an aura of righteousness in total contrast to the realities dictating them; and the UN emerged as a temple of official good intentions, a place where governments go to church, safely removed—by agreed untruth, procedural complexity, and sheer boredom—from the high risk of public involvement.

It was essential that the world's public be disengaged: the public, with its irreverent sharp questions, its appetite for exposure, its sporadic interest in justice, its vulgar curiosity regarding disbursement of its money. The UN enterprise was interpreted to populations through their governments. And between the institution and the public a buffer zone was laid out, of accredited well-wishers, whose role, on pain of treachery to world peace, was to put the organization's views to the world rather than force the world's emergencies on the organization. This protective screen was reinforced by theoreticians whose raison d'être derived from taking UN absurdities seriously; by those whose social strivings drew them to a place of luxury and incessant entertainments; and by accredited journalists as likely to reveal the organization's essence as a White House press corps to uncover Watergate. The public had no role in, or information on, the selection of UN leaders and was usually unaware of their existence prior to appointment.

Assemblies, councils, and committees provided the illusion of concern, emitting resolutions rarely implemented and documents seldom read. (UN headquarters alone now produces well over half a billion pages of words annually.) Such concerted action as did take place was that sanctioned by, and inevitable to, power politics and intergovernmental negotiation. As planetary emergencies intensified, so the sterile conference bodies and chaotic agencies of the UN proliferated—lest the rational impetus of survival, deprived of even these unproductive outlets, should take itself elsewhere and acquire force and coherence.

The public has little way of knowing, even now, that the mammoth UN congresses—such as those, in 1974, on the Law of the Sea and on Population—are a complex means of actually deferring urgent international actions while temporarily assuaging rising world apprehensions. The fixed pattern of these wasteful exercises is to disband with the sole explicit agreement of reconvening. Nor can citizens be aware that each new UN agency, such as that now proposed on the world food crisis, will inevitably be an institutional shambles—strangled at birth by national wire-pulling and impenetrable bureaucracy, incapacitated by corrupt appointments and monumental maladministration—with any achievement in gross disproportion to opportunity, emergency and vast expenditures of public funds.

In their anxiety to lull public inquiry, UN leaders have persistently misrepresented the organization's expenses by citing administrative costs only and suppressing operational ones. Thus the *New York Times* informed us recently that "the UN budget for the two-year period 1974–75 has been approved at $584,831,000."[4] This is like equating defense spending with Pentagon salaries. The actual UN budget for that period will be in the neighborhood of *four billion dollars*, exclusive of large national counterpart funds. (As to salaries, it may be mentioned that UN undersecretaries-general, who are thick on the ground, receive $65,000 per annum, exclusive of extensive allowances.)

Significantly, the public's original hopes of the organization have been consistently derided by the UN itself. The theme of a "jejune" world citizenry, placing utopian aspirations in international agencies, curiously recurs throughout UN histories and proclamations. Conversely, any reasonable inquirer into the UN's failures will find himself subjected to a barrage of statutory excuses bearing no relation whatever to humanity, logic, or survival.

Public expectations, which are standards in themselves and the very fuel of human progress, were annihilated in the scorched-earth policy by which world powers gained time for their own expedients. "Limited" wars, civil strife, and intranational subversion have multiplied, generally without UN comment. Vietnam and Cambodia have been torn to bloody shreds, virtually undiscussed at the United Nations. Repressive or unrepresentative regimes have on occasion been legitimized by the UN in the name of independence, while states such as Bangladesh have been refused nationhood until they claimed it by force. Every form of persecution and terrorism has proliferated while the UN Commission on Human Rights mired itself deeper in ludicrous procedures blatantly favoring governments, and deferred its agenda items for another year.

The invaluable lost ground of public expectation is not recoverable. Any future public call for global systems will not come as trust or aspiration but as an imperative, and to a violent accompaniment already being tuned.

The irresistible forces—social, political, economic, and Malthusian—that were denied rational expression at the United Nations went on, however, to manifest themselves in unprecedented levels of global crisis, in separate collective machinery, and in hugely powerful material forms remote from public knowledge or control. By creating, at the UN, a shrine of national sovereignty—"a United Governments Organization," as Solzhenitsyn calls it—where nationalism would be venerated long after its political and economic supremacy had dissipated, world power was free to bypass national structures with multinational operations far beyond the public field of vision.[5]

In the 1920s, H. G. Wells foresaw that world government might derive its missing authority from the global nature of modern science and commerce; and that this phenomenon, if exposed and seized upon in its early stages, could be channeled to the service of the world order. Reviewing Wells's *The World of William Clissold* in 1927, Keynes agreed that practical internationalism would absolutely require such an impetus, but pointed to the absence of any incentive to global outlook on the part of the captains of industry: "They lack altogether the kind of motive, the possession of which, if they had it, could be expressed by saying that they had a creed. They have no creed . . . [other than] money."[6]

Then and later, Keynes was—as Barnet and Müller point out in their recent *Global Reach*—"assuming a market in which national banks and national corporations transacted their business within the context of national boundaries."[7] It was Wells who glimpsed a future need of commercial forces to preserve and extend their global power without the inconsequential irruptions of nationalism. This prescience and this chance were cast away. Multinational commerce burgeoned, unregulated, as a new world despotism while, in the name of supranationalism, the dead horse of the United Nations was assiduously flogged between the shafts.

Mercantile powers were certainly long aware of the immediate advantages to themselves of neutralizing any effort at public jurisdiction over multinational activities. And the relation of corporation interests to the impotence of the United Nations is a vast question yet to be explored.

Occasional whiffs of sulfur rise from this region. In a volume of memoirs not otherwise conspicuous for candor, Lord Gladwyn remarks of the first UN secretary-general, Trygve Lie, what was well known to his unhappy staff at the time: "The people he liked associating with for the most part were American tycoons."[8] Billionaires in kindly mood have ever been banked around United Nations dinner tables and associated with the organization in its most innocuous "motherhood" aspect—and it may be noted that, through the bounty of John D. Rockefeller Jr., and Arthur Houghton Jr., respectively, the secretary-general's office premises and his residence are both provided by American industrialists.

A peculiarly squalid item of Lie's disastrous term was a collusion with IBM, through "one of Mr. Watson's top ranking assistants," to spy on and discredit the UN staff chairman—who, by no coincidence, was at the time exposing Lie's illicit collaborations with the State Department, the FBI, and Joseph McCarthy; and who was soon to be dismissed without cause. (The disgusting 1950 secret report on this matter from UN Chief of Protocol Jehan de Noue to Assistant Secretary-General Byron Price gives a succinct picture of United Nations hierarchy; and indeed deserves framing—a process with which it is, in another sense, closely associated.)

At the behest of oil companies, Dag Hammarskjöld suppressed circulation of a UN report on oil pricing in the 1950s. In 1968 a crucial revision of international law by the UN's Maritime Organization sanctioned deeper loading of tankers—an action immensely profitable to oil companies and calamitous to the ecology of oceans.[9] (True to the UN paradox, such a development supplies the perfect pendant to the UN Environment Program, suffocating in procedural restraints and internal discord in its skyscraper in Nairobi.) Corporation heads have successfully intervened through UN leaders to shape, to their own advantage, the forms of UN assistance to developing countries—for example, in modifying UN advice to new nations on negotiations with foreign investors. The head of the UN Development Program is no ecologically minded futurist but, traditionally, an American from the business world. (The incumbent, seventy-year-old Rudolph Peterson, is a former president to the Bank of America.)

It need only be added that an organ of the UN hypertrophy has the multinationals under "scrutiny."

This minefield will presumably be investigated eventually; along with such areas as the UN Secretariat's long, secret, and profoundly scandalous relations with national surveillance agencies such as the FBI.[10]

To maintain negativism on a moral pedestal is a feat of balance requiring auxiliaries. And to this end there developed, from the early days of the League [of Nations], that paradox within the paradox, the international civil servant: an essential but disregarded element in the failure of our international institutions: "The fact is, we are all going mad here—some quickly, some slowly, but all going the same way. . . . We shall do our work just as well, possibly better, when we are quite mad, and none of the governments will need to sacrifice any of their sane civil servants to take their places, and we shall continue to draw the pay."[11]

Thus, in 1928, League of Nations officials analyzed their functions in Alice Ritchie's admirable novel *The Peacemakers*. Closing his eyes to "a peculiarly abominable situation in the Near East," Miss Ritchie's ineffectual secretary-general (a portrait of Sir Eric Drummond) vaguely wonders, "What was the good of the [league] if it placed self-preservation before its plain duty? He did not know; it was hardly his province. He was there to keep it in being."[12] And the league was of course defunct a dozen years later.

This moral lesson was lost on the persuaded apostles of negativism for whom the United Nations civil service has been such a magnet; but not, by any means, on the organization's member states. The lengths to which governments have gone to preclude the hair-shirt Secretariat (nominally decreed by the UN Charter) make exquisite irony of the everlasting chant of UN leaders that they are necessarily the pawns of national pressures. Illicit recruitment clearances, dehumanization, retributions, rewards, and a flooding of the upper echelons with biased and incompetent national appointees guarantee that the United Nations will never acquire that incalculable power generated by the assumption of responsibility.

Rationalizations of UN inaction have grown ever more grotesque in the face of world events. In the past year there has been a marked effort by UN leaders to characterize the ancient principles of law and common humanity set forth in the UN Charter and Universal Declaration of Human Rights as cultural sophistries of the Western world—as narrow concepts, in fact, that the UN is too large-minded to apply indiscriminately. Over the title of "Spokesman for the Secretary-General," the UN's André Lewin qualified his sworn support for freedom of information ("by this I mean fair information"), as follows:

> I do not feel, however, that belonging to the Western world and adhering to its ideology, I should impose my point of view on an organization where many countries have different conceptions, ideologies and interests. . . . I do not feel that an organization representing billions of people, for whom freedom of information has not the same meaning and importance as for westerners, should work according to western standards. . . . We should try to find and follow a way in the middle.[13]

This theory of the golden mean as a justification for abrogating basic standards of course originates with governments, who enthusiastically promote the view that populations unable to articulate their grievances are not desirous of redressing them. In the field of information, the "way in the middle" has recently led to UN censorship against Solzhenitsyn and Confucius.

United Nations archives are a repository of hundreds of thousands of unavailing petitions to the world custodians of human rights. Amnesty International has, over the years, submitted thousands of documented cases of persecution to the UN without receiving action on one of them. In 1973 UNESCO withdrew facilities from an Amnesty conference protesting torture lest offense be given to governments engaged in that activity.[14] A few weeks later, the UN Human Rights Commission made a backstage agreement to play down torture in Chile in exchange for silence on Solzhenitsyn and the Soviet dissidents.[15] In this area of human rights, above all, the organs have been mercilessly employed to thwart mankind's natural expressions of pity, decency and civilization.

On the apparent assumption of "better too late than never," the City University of New York has recently issued a study of the political strangulation of the United Nations Secretariat.[16] As stated by its authors, it is limited in scope, although this would not account for fundamental omissions and errors. It is indicative that this report, which emanates from the UN buffer zone, does not even consider the relation of citizens to the United Nations: the public is mentioned only in passing, as the passive recipient of a UN "image."[17] The United Nations budget is given, yet again, only in administrative costs (as "$225 million").[18] And so on. What *is* present, and accurate, is doubtless well worth saying over again for the record. The illusion, however, that the deeply intended disorder of the UN Augean stables can be set to rights by the cosmetic measures, now thirty years overdue, enumerated in this report cannot be indulged. It is inherently impossible for the United Nations to embrace the administrative atonement prescribed in this and similar parochial studies, nor will events permit of any such improbable and time-consuming reversal.

Some years ago I wrote that "the present United Nations is a veritable haystack of last straws, without resilience for the unexpected."[19]

Since then, world convulsions have brought the UN back into public view. Though confusedly related to recent shocks, the public's current disillusionment with the United Nations arises also from a cumulative awareness of the organization's unreality amid contemporary events. Governments, whatever their bluster, will not want the dissolution of an institution that must, in this global era, be in some manner reconstituted to their disadvantage; and the highly dubious billion-dollar UN refuge under construction at Vienna testifies to huge vested interests in the status quo. It is for the public to insist that the present travesty be superseded, at this eleventh hour, by responsive world systems.

"There is," said Machiavelli quoting Dante, "no order without knowledge of the past."[20] It may be added that exposure sets in motion its own solutions.

THE LEAGUE OF FRIGHTENED MEN

Why the UN Is so Useless

> To act with doubleness towards a man whose own conduct was double, was so near an approach to virtue that it deserved to be called by no meaner name than diplomacy.
>
> —George Eliot, *Felix Holt, the Radical*

Something like this view of George Eliot's may have influenced Iranian leaders in their contemptuous dismissal of Kurt Waldheim last week in Tehran.[1] There was no reason for any of the prevailing factions in Iran to negotiate with an official who had ignored the atrocities of the previous regime, and had made himself an eager instrument of the shah's policy of buying respectability through donations to overseas institutions. Year after year, as Amnesty International presented documented reports of gross violations in Iran, the United Nations Secretariat—supposed custodian of human rights—courted funds from the shah and, in return, helped him to furbish his image.

Returning from Tehran, an unnerved Waldheim appeared on ABC's *Issues and Answers*. He indignantly denied that the United Nations had done nothing about the abuses of the shah and SAVAK [secret police]. "I received hundreds and thousands of complaints, and we always dealt with them. We sent them to the . . . [Waldheim pauses here]—and I even spoke to the Iranians. When I was in Iran two years ago, I did raise the question, but the then authorities said they wouldn't discuss the matter with me."[2] This tragic charade—referring reports of atrocities back to the offending government for consideration—is indeed standard UN procedure. It is augmented by the UN Commission on Human Rights, a discredited body presided over for a time by Princess Ashraf, the sister of the shah.

Princess Ashraf recently placed a full-page ad in some American newspapers to remind Waldheim about his past appreciation of her brother's favors.[3] Her tactless *aide-memoire* included a photograph of a jubilant Waldheim clutching the princess with one hand and a large Pahlavi check with the other. It quoted rhapsodic tributes to the humanitarian ideas of the Pahlavis from Waldheim and his assistant, Mrs. Helvi Sipila. Princess Ashraf chaired a variety of UN rights bodies in the 1970s, and was given a leading role in the chaotic International Women's Conference held at Mexico City in 1975 and made possible by Iranian munificence. Until events overtook them, there were plans for a UN training institute for women in Iran, with a proposed Iranian budget of one million dollars. Despite this seeming preoccupation with women's rights, Kurt Waldheim demonstrated massive discrimination against women within his own staff. Princess Ashraf showed no support for the Iranian women who bravely marched in thousands last year in Tehran to protest repression by the ayatollah.

During the shah's ascendancy, Waldheim administered an annual award of $50,000, known as the Pahlavi Prize, paid for by guess-who and conferred for environmental services.[4] The first recipient was Waldheim's own colleague, Maurice Strong, who was leaving the UN Environment Program after a short and turbulent career.[5]

When Kurt Waldheim set foot in Iran on New Year's Day, his first utterance was characteristically negative: "You cannot expect from such a first visit to solve immediately all problems. That is not being realistic."[6] Much more unrealistic was his supposition that the world observed the capers of UN officials with any residual optimism. Last October [1979], the *Guardian* of London discussed Waldheim's role (nonexistent) in ending the Cambodia tragedy: "As so often when anything important is taking place in the world, the UN itself is silent.

It is aided, abetted and guided in that silence by the inactivity of the Secretary-General himself. . . . Why does not Kurt Waldheim make a strenuous effort to overcome the deadly punctilio in which his office has taken refuge?"[7]

In fact, the deadly punctilio is organic. The method for selecting Secretariat leaders is the only UN official process that can be described as finely honed. United Nations senior officers are systematically chosen for their very lack of moral courage and independent mind. The office of secretary-general is the pinnacle on which this negative capability culminates. In Waldheim, the position has found its consummate expression.

Kurt Waldheim was born in Austria in 1918. He came to manhood, as it were, with the Anschluss, dutifully following the normal path by taking part in the Nazi youth movement and serving in Hitler's army in various campaigns including the Eastern Front. To do otherwise would have been to exhibit a rare heroism—and, incidentally, to disqualify himself, had he survived, for the future position of UN secretary-general. Unflawed by any such aberration, Waldheim moved on through the Austrian diplomatic service and foreign ministry into the political life of his country, apparently intent on gaining high office. In 1971, shortly before his installation as UN secretary-general, he was an unsuccessful candidate for the Austrian presidency. His UN appointment was sought, and possibly attained, through intensive lobbying.

When Waldheim's predecessor, the Burmese U Thant, retired as secretary-general, it was—as was remarked of Asquith's fall from power—as if a pin had dropped. Waldheim inherited from Thant a position steeped in self-righteous timidity and administrative incapacity. The first UN secretary-general, Trygve Lie—whose background as a labor lawyer and member of Norway's wartime government-in-exile might have promised better—had demolished any germ of a true international civil service by conspiring to violate the charter before its ink was dry. In the UN's infancy, Lie contracted a secret agreement with the US government whereby Washington was given control over UN administrative procedures. The United States used this control to dominate the secretariat for twenty years, with incalculable adverse effect on UN potential, and in the end with particularly negative results for the United States.

The most powerful member of the UN Secretariat in the organization's formative years was not Trygve Lie but the administrative chief, Byron Price, an American of destructive tendencies who was in effect Washington's chief covert agent at UN headquarters. During the McCarthy years, the Secretariat administration expelled, repelled, persecuted, intimidated, or alienated virtually every free-thinking employee in its senior and intermediate grades. This left a dross from which the present administrative edifice was formed. The danger to be avoided, in the view of member governments, was the possibility that a truly international civil service might be created, in accordance with the provisions of the UN Charter, to represent the moral principles that governments were likely to ignore. The organization was convulsed over this issue for six years. Lie's legal officer, an American, committed suicide; and Lie himself, along with Byron Price, eventually resigned—but not before they had installed a branch of the US Federal Bureau of Investigation at UN headquarters, on international territory, for the purpose of "screening" the staff. The FBI office was retained by Dag Hammarskjöld until it had completed its "task." No senior UN official was heard to object.

Despite its systematic exclusion of persons of character from the Secretariat, and its rejection of candidates with even a mild show of unorthodoxy in their backgrounds, the UN administration has knowingly recruited, and retained in prolonged employment at senior grades, agents of the KGB and CIA—and, presumably, of every other national secret police on earth. That is entirely consistent with a UN precept that the only unforgivable offense a senior official can commit is to lose the endorsement of the relevant member government—not necessarily his own. When the double agent Shevchenko defected to the United States last year from his high UN post, it was announced that even though he had violated every contractual obligation, his UN pension would be paid.[8] The former head of the UN mission in Cyprus, Prince Alfred zur Lippe-Weissenfeld, who resigned last September after repeated complaints from the government about his massive thefts of Cypriot antiquities, also will receive his UN annuity.[9]

Waldheim's own past presented no obstacle to his UN appointment. When the United Nations was founded, former members of fascist organizations in the belligerent states were declared ineligible for UN service. But this prohibition was rescinded quietly in 1952, at the very time when rigorous provisions were introduced against infusions of nonconformity. To have embraced a status quo, fascist or otherwise, apparently connoted the desired team mentality. What the United Nations abhorred was individual distinction. This view follows the precedent set in the 1930s by the League of Nations, whose officials declined to recognize the plight of German and Austrian Jews.

The field of human rights is where the United Nations Secretariat had, and cast away, its supreme opportunity. In the intensifying violence of the last three decades, UN bodies of human rights and the leaders of the UN Secretariat have remained virtually silent: about American ravages in Asia, and about Pol Pot; about genocide in Biafra and Indonesia, starvation in Ethiopia, torture in Greece, Chile, Argentina, Guatemala, the Philippines, and Uganda; about punitive mutilation in Saudi Arabia, and about the vast prison network of the Soviet Union.

Into the vacuum created by UN inaction on human rights has come an active humanitarianism by individuals and private agencies that has gradually formed itself into a moral force—a force of the kind that a different United Nations might have inspired and led. This is the most hopeful development of the past decade. Organizations like Amnesty International operate with voluntary contributions: they offer their workers no exorbitant salaries or inane revels, and no delusions of self-importance. Nevertheless, they mobilize inestimable resources of human fellowship and proper indignation, and have assumed the task that the United Nations, with its colossal funds and massive bureaucracy, would not attempt. Only since the human rights movement burgeoned into a force not to be ignored has the United Nations made any effort to overcome its own paralysis in this area. Even so, Amnesty International has received no action on any of the thousands of documented cases it has submitted to the United Nations over many years.

In his Nobel address, Aleksandr Solzhenitsyn denounced the United Nations as a place where individuals have no voice or right of appeal:

> It is not a United Nations organization but a United Governments organization . . . which has cravenly set itself against investigating private grievances—the groans, cries, and entreaties of single, simple individuals . . . and abandoned ordinary persons to the mercy of regimes not of their choosing.[10]

Solzhenitsyn cannot address the United Nations. Terrorists bearing arms can address UN assemblies, but not the moral heroes and martyrs of our violent age. The only notable recognition of his existence that Solzhenitsyn has received from the United Nations was a clandestine attempt by Waldheim and his associates, at the Soviets' behest, to suppress his works in commercial bookshops on UN territory. Meanwhile in Moscow, in September 1977, Waldheim presented Leonid Brezhnev with the UN peace medal, "in recognition of his considerable and fruitful activities in favor of universal peace and people's security."[11]

Each December a handful of Soviet citizens demonstrate to commemorate the promulgation of the UN Universal Declaration of Human Rights. They are inevitably and invariably arrested by the Soviet police within moments of their appearance.[12] No UN medals have ever been conferred on them, nor has a UN official ever publicly raised a voice on their behalf.

The UN Secretariat is a disordered and hypertrophic institution whose continuance, as a UN official recently remarked, "defies the laws of logic and gravity."[13] This is reflected in the quality of all UN services, most tragically in the conception and execution of relief programs and technological aid. A systematic public inquiry into the competence of UN management and its cost effectiveness is overdue. It would be interesting to compare the true proportion of the budget spent on administrative costs in UN projects to that in private relief agencies. The US Senate Committee on Government Operations [since 2004 the Senate Committee on Homeland Security and Governmental Affairs] found in 1977 that UN salaries and material benefits ran 50 percent to 650 percent higher than the corresponding rewards to US civil servants.[14]

Any effort to shed light on this pleonexia is characterized by the United Nations as a blow to world peace. Generally it arouses the only show of moral outrage at which UN circles excel. In the past year, realistic reporting on the United Nations by Morton Mintz of the *Washington Post* and a series in the same paper by Ronald Kessler about UN finances brought hysterical denunciation from both the United Nations and the US State Department. Charles Maynes, assistant secretary of state for international organizations, confirmed that Kessler's statistics were accurate, but told the *Post* that "an article on the overall financial situation of the UN system would be used unfairly by political critics of the United Nations." Maynes said that a story on the subject "will do tremendous damage to the United Nations. . . . The damage will be incredible. It will be devastating."[15] And so on.

United Nations officials were not called upon to testify at the cursory congressional inquiry that followed the *Post* story because, as a congressional aide explained, "the United Nations prohibits its employees from testifying before a member country's legislative committees."[16] As it happens, dozens of American UN employees did appear many years ago before the McCarran Internal Security Subcommittee, which made political sport of them and ruined their careers. Not only did the UN administration make no objection to this procedure, but it made clear that any employee who refused the summons would be dismissed.[17]

It is hard to see how significant reform of the present UN system could ever be effected. In any case, a juster system, based on merit as decreed by the UN Charter, could not be introduced without scuttling the corrupt political basis of the present bureaucracy. It is among the intermediate and junior staff of the United Nations that decency has lingered, like a trace of archaic culture in a totalitarian state. The extirpations of early years silenced resistance for a generation; and the staff in general remains an extremely conditioned and intimidated group. Nevertheless, with the entry of younger people into the lower and middle grades, where appointments are not yet exclusively dictated by governments, some courage has filtered back.

The labor mediator Theodor Kheel recently has undertaken, for a nominal fee, to represent the UN staff in its struggle with the administration. Kheel says that he has never encountered anything approaching the UN administration's authoritarian attitude in forty years of labor mediation, and compares the UN leadership to "the court of Henry VIII." Kheel says, "Waldheim would be a better international mediator if he'd eschew the role of ayatollah toward his own staff."[18]

When Pliable, in *The Pilgrim's Progress*, turned back at the Slough of Despond and found his way home, he was at first "held greatly in derision among all sorts of people."[19] But soon he recovered confidence. In Waldheim's case, too, with his recent excursion to Iran, the hollowness of his office has been only briefly exposed. But the question of Waldheim's reelection is imminent, and the Iranian debacle—which has yet to run its course—may put an end to his UN career. This could provide an opportunity for the public, for the first time, to observe and criticize the appointment of his successor.

Throughout the modern world, fear has created a heightened consciousness of human rights. The rise of active human rights agencies outside the United Nations suggests the form that a future world body might take. Whether public apprehension can be engaged toward the creation of rational international instruments depends, to a large extent, on serious treatment of this theme in the world's press, where it has as yet been little explored. Having almost no realistic information on the United Nations, the public cannot frame hard questions, and takes the organization at the UN's own trivial valuation, as an innocuous captive of incompatible national demands.

UNHELPFUL

Waldheim's Latest Debacle

At Tehran, in 1968, the United Nations held an International Conference on Human Rights, with funds and facilities provided by the shah. The shah himself delivered the opening address on the sanctity of human rights. The shah's sister Princess Ashraf presided over the conference. The United Nations secretary-general, U Thant, in thanking "His Imperial Majesty" for his beneficence, found it "very fitting" that the conference should take place in Iran, and went on to condemn "massacres, tortures, arbitrary arrests, cruel detentions, and summary executions" in far-flung and unspecified areas of the globe.[1]

Over decades of the shah's rule, UN organs availed themselves of special donations from the Pahlavis for costly and unproductive verbal exercises in the promulgation of "rights," and in return enabled Pahlavi nominees to preside over numerous UN human rights gatherings.[2] Throughout that time, UN officials mercilessly ignored a huge body of verified information on political persecutions and atrocities in Iran, and many thousands of appeals from the shah's victims. In accordance with UN procedure, such appeals were either referred back to the offending government for "comment" or considered by the UN Commission on Human Rights—over which ineffable body Princess Ashraf for a time presided.

In March 1980 the recently established UN commission of inquiry returned from Iran empty-handed, leaving behind the American hostages as well as their own expressions of horror at the shah's atrocities.

The commission assured mutilated survivors that "the international community will know to what unimaginable lengths the violations of human rights were carried in this land. . . . Your sacrifice will not have been in vain."[3] Commission member Adib Daoudy of Syria, who has proclaimed that approximately 90,000 people died in the shah's torture chambers (though he headed Syria's delegation to Tehran in 1968), declared: "It's awful. It's dreadful."[4]

Despite such protestations, the UN's unwillingness to deliver on its promises remains unchanged. In January, Secretary-General Waldheim left Tehran promising to "do whatever we can to ensure that this mutilation of human beings will never take place again." Yet once safely home, Waldheim expressed through his wife—in a grotesque interview with the *Washington Post*—his determination never to say "a bad word about the shah. Whatever he did was his problem."[5]

In keeping with the modern revolutionary pattern, "rights" emptily promised have been claimed in deadly earnest. The UN, far from being "our best hope for peace," has contributed to the escalating violence and violation by its refusal to give any effective voice to the grievances of populations, minorities, or individuals.[6]

Acting at the direction of its member governments, the UN has a capital interest in preventing political complainants from obtaining a proper hearing, let alone redress. United Nations performance in the human rights field since the organization's inception plainly shows that UN "rights" organs have been maintained to short-circuit charges of government abuse and to screen violations from public view—as in Iran in 1968, where the babble in the conference hall was employed to drown out unseemly sounds from the adjoining torture-chamber; or, as in the case of Chile in the period following Allende's death, when an East-West bargain was struck in the UN Human Rights Commission to minimize reports of torture in Chile in exchange for silence on Soviet dissidents.[7]

The few—and so far largely procedural—improvements in the recent performance of the UN Human Rights Commission are related to the emergence, and contrasting efficacy, of private rights groups such as Amnesty International, which, together with the very intensification of world violence, have increasingly exposed UN delinquency.

Like all UN organs, the UN bureaucracy is subservient to the demands of national authorities, whatever their insensitivity to explicit UN principles. Kurt Waldheim felt able to extol the Pahlavis' "humanitarian ideals" and able to ignore their atrocities as long as the shah was acknowledged head of a munificent UN member government—supported by the United States, a member nation more powerful still. With the shah's fall, "authority" in Iran devolved on the present factions, and the UN leadership, in unabashed reversal, declared its moral outrage and set up its commission of inquiry. Were the Pahlavis to regain power, we might expect to see—under the UN Vicar-of-Bray syndrome—a UN tribunal investigating the plentiful abuses of the ayatollah. I have seen no suggestion that the UN commission of inquiry might more usefully have been set up while the shah's abuses were in progress in Iran, although this is precisely the type of investigation undertaken, with scant funds at considerable risk, by private human rights agencies.

Far from displaying humility over his misstatements and failures in the Iranian crisis, Kurt Waldheim "expressed scorn," according to the *New York Times*, "for critics who, in his view, had not devised any other approach. 'Nobody has offered me any alternative.'"[8] This critic has in fact been proposing, for a decade, specific measures by which the UN Secretariat could set about acquiring, however tardily, the stature and credibility needed for effective mediation. Every thinking member of the UN staff is aware that proper alternatives to UN debility propose themselves daily and are repudiated by the UN administration as incompatible with the corrupt forms in which the organization has established itself.

The UN has set itself against recognizing, let alone profiting from, the context in which the Iranian experience is taking place. Just as, at a recent press conference, Jimmy Carter dismissed as "ancient history" a question as to whether current events demonstrated past errors in American policy in Iran, so the UN cultivates amnesia toward its own responsibility.[9] "Responsibility" is not a word in use at the UN.

Over the past year or two, deputations of concerned UN employees have approached the "more serious" member governments, through their UN mission, in an attempt to gain support for essential reforms. The response of these governments may be summarized as follows: we are aware of the deplorable condition of the UN Secretariat, and of its adverse effect on the organization's under taking: but we are not disposed to make—in the words of one representative—"the expenditure of political capital necessary to effect the required reforms."[10] In other words, the United Nations' ineffectuality, so deeply the product of governmental intentions, will continue to satisfy even its "more serious" members until global violence passes the bounds of any conceivable form of international mediation. This attitude, however, assumes that UN services can be allowed to deteriorate indefinitely without attracting public attention, and that the UN staff body will continue to tolerate a degree of maladministration and injustice scarcely definable as civilized. In fact, the government of Belgium is transferring its contribution for Cambodian relief from the UN to effective private agencies, such as Oxfam.[11]

Analogous to the Iranian hostage crisis is the case of a UN international employee, Alicja Wesolowska, a secretary of Polish nationality arrested last August at Warsaw en route to a UN assignment. Deprived of her elementary rights, as well as those due her as an international civil servant, Wesolowska was held in solitary confinement until her trial in March, when she was sentenced to seven year's imprisonment for "espionage," a charge for which there is no concrete evidence. Wesolowska's captivity and trial have taken place in flagrant violation of international conventions to which the Polish government is a signatory. In her case, however, the UN administration has shown itself not only helpless but reluctant to respond with any public assertion of a principle vital to its own survival. And a staff appeal for initiation of procedures to take the case to the World Court has so far received no action.

Concern among UN staff over the Wesolowska matter has brought to light a number of other cases of UN employees who have been arbitrarily arrested while performing UN duties; and who, in some cases, are presumed to have died in prison. No visible effort has been made by the UN administration on their behalf. As a UN official explained to a concerned inquirer, "They are all junior employees."[12] And no powerful government is exercised over their fate.

No significant reform of the UN can occur without a profound change in the quality of UN press coverage. Reporting on the UN is traditionally indulgent to the point of infantilism, and sometimes indistinguishable from the vast propaganda apparatus maintained at public expense by the UN itself. In the case of Iran in particular, there is apparently no attempt by the press to relate UN failures to their larger context, nor any evidence of independent research. Waldheim's discomfiture at Tehran in January was connected, by the UN press, to nothing more substantial than his once having kissed Princess Ashraf's hand.[13]

While the UN commission of inquiry was being formed, portentous UN bulletins were prominent in each day's newspapers. On an evident assumption that Iranians cannot read, reassurances emanated from the UN to the press to the effect that the UN inquiry would be merely "cosmetic," and "would enable Iran's new government to tell its people that their complaints have received international sanction and thus permit the authorities to free the captives."[14] The *New York Times* relayed that "United Nations officials are making little pretense that they have suddenly been overcome with shock and remorse over the shah's regime; rather, the Commission's investigation is seen as a device to get the hostages released."[15]

Waldheim was described—presumably according to a UN definition of intrepidity—as having "taken a great risk"; and a timeworn UN formula of strength through incompetence was exhumed in the claim, solemnly relayed, that "the United Nations' very lack of precision, its fuzzy improvisation, are precisely the qualities needed to fit the complex politics and unsettled internal power struggles in Iran."[16]

As realities obtruded, front-page assertions gave way to more obscurely placed references to "delicate negotiations."[17] With the collapse of the commission's effort, reporting dwindled to uncritical reflections on the confused and inscrutable factions competing for power in Iran; with still no attempt to explore the confusions of the distinctly scrutable UN.

It seems probable, at this time, that the hostages at Tehran eventually will be released. Iran has pressing reasons, internal and external, to settle the matter. The journalist who brings the true condition of the UN before the public will make history. He will also pave the way for revision of international organizations. Jimmy Carter and Kurt Waldheim [d. 2007] are facing their respective reelections and, in their urgent need for political capital, can be expected to exert their utmost efforts to resolve the impasse at Tehran. It is idle, however, to pretend that Waldheim—insofar as he retains a role—has a humanitarian stake in the fate of the hostages. Nothing in the past conduct of his office, particularly as it refers to Iran, suggests such a concern.

A WRITER'S REFLECTIONS ON THE NUCLEAR AGE

The first news of the atomic bomb reached Australia on a winter morning—I suppose it was the day following the event. I was dressing to go to school and heard the announcement on the radio. I hardly know why the moment was immediately understood to be important—anesthetized as we were by six years of information on mass bombing throughout Europe and in Asia. Even then, in the brute climate of war, there were persons who began to ponder the consequences—material, ethical, psychological, self-evident, or subtle. I was not close to such people, but the debate opened quickly and was already a global preoccupation by the time the tests took place at Bikini Atoll.

Twenty months after the bomb was dropped, I was at Hiroshima. I was en route to Hong Kong, where my father was taking a government job. We had traveled from Sydney to Japan in a tiny ship, taking over a month on the way and stopping only once, briefly, for water in New Guinea. The ship was carrying about fifty wives of Australian officers in the occupation force in Japan. Some of these women had been parted from their husbands for the duration of the war. We arrived at the port of Kure, which was a shambles from the bombardment, and spent the next day at Hiroshima, a short drive distant. The city center was still a wasteland, quite empty apart from the mangled dome and blitzed shreds even then familiar to us from photographs. On the outskirts, a lot of rebuilding was taking place: new houses swiftly assembled from light timber and plywood. Men and women were engaged in this busy scene, while the cast central area of the bombing remained still and empty, like a gray lake. The attitude of my family and of the officers accompanying us was the conventional one: that the bomb was an inevitable and justified—and even merciful—outcome of the total war. Yet among these generally unreflective people there was some uneasiness in discussing it. No one could explain why the bomb had not, in the first instance at least, been dropped in an unpopulated place. That was the extent of objection.

A recurrent theme at the time was that such a weapon would come to be "like gas" in the First World War—impossible to deploy from fear of retaliation in kind. No one I knew had yet envisaged the immensely more destructive hydrogen bomb, or the stockpiling of thousands of such devices. In other words, we had not then recognized that self-destructive tendencies in world leadership—and, by extension, in mankind—would prove stronger than rational fear or instincts of self-preservation.

I was, by my generation, part of the new world. But I had been raised in the climate of war, not only from having passed my late childhood and early adolescence in years of world war but from being born—as were all my contemporaries, British or Australian—into consciousness of "the Great War." The lingering pity and horror of the 1914–18 war pervaded and in some measure dominated our lives, along with the visible misery of the Depression. My father had been in the trenches in France at the age of seventeen. In a way, this led to our early acceptance of battle as, in Mussolini's terrible words, "the natural condition of man," and I had never heard either of the great wars discussed in anything other than a context of patriotism and righteousness. However, I think now that the immense presence of the First World War in the thought and life of the decades between wars was indicative of doubts already raised in the unconscious mind. I never heard that war discussed in a casual way by its veterans (as I have, for example, heard later veterans relate incidents of the war of 1939–45). The scale of horror had been too new, too vast. The next change of dimension came, I think, with the atom bomb. The intervening horrors, of the Second World War, had to some extent been anticipated by human imagination. But not the bomb.

The world conditions in which the atomic bomb was dropped can hardly be re-created in the mind. In Australia, we had recently and narrowly escaped Japanese invasion. Japanese bombs had fallen on Australian soil. Japanese submarines had entered—and briefly bombarded—the harbor of Sydney. Like thousands of other schoolchildren, I had been an evacuee. Thousands of Australians had spent years in Japanese prison camps, and many had died there in atrocious conditions. Nearly every able-bodied man in the land had gone to war, and the casualty lists were long. The animus of revenge in war is powerful, and it is merged with the—more rational—sense of deliverance.

Some weeks ago an Australian friend—a poet and entirely gentle person—visited us in New York. We spoke in despair of the neutron bomb, with which Reagan had just announced his intention to proceed. The poet mentioned his own "first memory" of the atomic bomb. He had been a soldier at the time and dying of wounds in a makeshift jungle hospital on a remote Pacific island. His unit had learned it was hopelessly outnumbered by Japanese troops a few miles away. With the news of the bomb, they were saved. He said, "I never knew how to handle this in my mind: I wish the bomb had never been invented, let alone dropped. But if it had not been, I would be a rotting skeleton these thirty-odd years."

The fallout of the bomb on our modern thought and life has been continuous and incalculable. And combined over the same period, with other destructive phenomena that exist on a new, incomparable scale: pollution of air, water, oceans, upper atmosphere; the death of forests, of species; the depletion of natural resources and essential minerals; overpopulation and threat of world famine; dislocation of entire peoples; and the apparent disintegration of structures of civilized order. It is impossible to be confident of "posterity." Even were we assured of the survival of the race, we could not prefigure to ourselves the forms of future human existence or its qualities of mind. In our present uncertainty, not the least danger lies, too, in self-dramatization: our state of suspense is exploited, on the one hand, to excuse inertia; and, on the other, to justify violence.

I have written, briefly, in fiction, on Hiroshima and the bomb. In my own life, the event was a confused beginning of pacifism. And also of an awareness that immense evils are impossible to hold in the mind. One's own contemplation of them can carry dangers of posturing, of easy vehemence, and of claims of unearned morality. By contrast, acts of goodness—even of "public" goodness—can only be properly discussed or understood in their individual manifestations. The dominant proposition of the atomic age—that humankind is doomed by its own evil—cannot be refuted with any single sweeping show of virtue analogous to the bomb. To counter the implications of the bomb, humanity can only offer its history of individual gestures—the proofs of decency, pity, integrity, and independent courage. I suppose this touches the central premise of the Christian ideal, and the very meaning of the word Redeemer. However, the sense of it as a reality was formed in me long before I realized that and was developed by a few great living spirits I have been lucky enough to know.

I cannot prevent the making of the bomb—although, like others, I may make my protest. I cannot prevent the use of it. My faith is, merely, that the world against which the bomb may be used has not entirely deserved it.

PART 4

The Great Occasion

CANTON MORE FAR

The hotel at the corner of Des Voeux Road and Pedder Street in Hong Kong used to be called the Gloucester. (It has now been remodeled, I believe, and is no longer a hotel.) From the terraces of its higher floors, in the years immediately after the Second World War, one overlooked the busiest intersection in the city, for it was at this crossroads that the trams of Des Voeux Road joined battle with the traffic of Pedder Street and Chater Road, and no detail of the ensuing holocaust was lost on the patrons of the Gloucester. Little black English cars, outnumbered, fought for their rights with bright new American ones. (Studebakers, which formed the taxi population, were a great joke to the British colony, being as long in back as in front and giving the appearance of going both ways.) Rickshaws and pedicabs swerved in and out of the struggle, the rickshaw coolies sending up urgent cries for room to maintain the rhythm of their stride. The tram bells clanged, the small black cars snorted, the big bright ones gave screams of delight, and every so often an expressionless colonial policeman—a Chinese in white tropical uniform and black Sam Brown belt—would rise up in the middle and give the signal for the pedestrians to charge. Into the melee then surged an excited crowd in which every known nationality and profession was represented—colonial Englishwomen in linen dresses and wedge heels, Chinese women in silk sheaths and platform soles, British soldiers, American sailors, businessmen in white duck, tourists from the American President Lines upholstered in seersucker and cameras, White Russians looking tragic, Indians looking vague, amahs in pajamas, beggars in fearful states of disintegration, and an endless stream of coolies at a trot carrying an endless variety of heavy weights on poles.

Because of the placing of the hotel at a crossroads, a number of vistas opened up to the eye thankfully lifted from the dizzy scene below. On the Pedder Street side, the hotel looked across to peeling gray stucco on the arcades and pilasters of Jardine Matheson & Co.—a business establishment of long history and large influence in the East. The upper verandahs of Jardine's, which were glassed in the following year to provide more offices, were still open in 1947, and many a pleasant and promising young imperialist was to be seen strolling there in the early afternoon—after tiffin, as lunch was sometimes called—across the cracked tiles and fallen plaster that showed the effects of recent war.

The lower part of Des Voeux Road, below the Pedder Street crossing, soon became almost exclusively Chinese, a welter of shops, stalls, restaurants, and warrenlike businesses, so that this view of the street was a forest of colorful signs in Chinese characters, rising from the dust-clouded traffic of the road. Above the crossing, on the other hand, Des Voeux Road was conventionality itself—a wide and well-paved avenue that curved for half a mile in an arc of pretty shops, cafes, offices, and banks, and eventually emptied itself into the Cricket Ground as surely as a great river must find its way to the sea.

Back at the Gloucester, one looked diagonally across to the General Post Office. This remarkable consummation of colonial architecture had been festooned by its creators with all manner of pinnacles, cornices, false buttresses, blank balconies, gargoyles, and goddesses—a triumph of matter over mind. Beyond the post office one glimpsed the sea, surmounted by the busy Praya. (In Hong Kong one cannot turn one's head without seeing either the harbor or the green mountain along whose foot the city lies.) In Des Voeux Road—that is, in its respectable direction—was the prow of yet another arcaded and stuccoed colonial building. This prow, although it went by the cozy name of Watson's Corner, was in fact rounded and glazed, its principal monument being the chemist's shop for which it was named. As one approached Watson's Corner from the Gloucester, its convex semicircle of glassed-in arches gave the building a cheerful effect of grinning from ear to ear.

If you were sixteen at that time and living in an Eastern city with your parents, your main sensation would probably have been, as mine was, one of enforced detachment, for, while encouraged to observe, you were forbidden to participate. Though constantly enjoined to appreciate your opportunity, you were forbidden to seize it. I spent a great deal of time leaning on the rail of our hotel balcony. If I descended, it was en route to a tennis or tea party, or to decorous dances on board reassuringly British ships of war in the harbor where I learned the difference between a sloop and a destroyer. The Gloucester intersection was my first sight of what is called the real world (that is, the world you imagine to exist rather than the one you actually inhabit), and, having for many months no more profitable occupation, I was set beside it in a way that an invalid is put by a window—to enjoy a spectacle in which he may play no part.

On the colony's social map at that time the principal elevations were Government House, where the governor lived; Flagstaff House, where the general lived; and Admiralty House, which sheltered the admiral. It was at the last-named of these, one evening, that I was fascinated by an arrangement of small, circular board and wooden mallet that the admiral—who sat at the middle rather than the end of his table—kept beside his wineglass. All through dinner I speculated on its function, fearing (for the adult world was already revealing its affinities with school) that it was reserved for the delivery of some humiliating reprimand. Ultimately, the Stilton, fruit, and cabinet pudding having been successively removed by a multitude of servants, a silence fell. The admiral took up the mallet and struck the board a single resounding blow. He then announced, "Gentlemen, you may now smoke." This was the signal for the ladies to withdraw.

In those days it was always a toss-up with me whether I would be overawed or have a fit of the giggles. This time I was awed.

I am told that many of the landmarks I have described no longer exist, that there have been many additions and substitutions, and that I would not recognize the place. In my case, too, there have been many changes, and the place might not recognize me. Maybe our conditions have not so much been altered as intensified.

Hong Kong in those postwar years was a stepping stone in a quicksand—a safe place from which to go to places less secure. If one wanted a change, one could go to Shanghai, or to Nanking, where the capital then was, or to Peiping (by air, since the civil war had already made the train trip precarious, and the city was in a sense besieged). In my case, so it was said, such a trip made alone would be unthinkable. I did think of it, though, quite often; but for a long time remained planted at the Gloucester with both elbows on the balcony railing.

Inconclusive attempts were made to place me in the ruined shell of the Hong Kong University or under the wing of the French Jesuit school. At one time I was to be packed off to a school in England, but a terrible winter there intervened to save me. What was needed was an occupation—an occupation being distinguished from a job in that it involves fewer qualifications, a lower salary, and makes no pretensions to career—and this was eventually found for me.

My occupation was in a place of authority—of high and confidential authority—an office concerned with the colony's security. Regarding my own task there, however, there need be no secrecy. I was charged with the placing of flagged pins on a map, each pin representing a merchant ship and the map being that of Far Eastern waters. The ships voluntarily gave their positions at regular intervals for this purpose, and the idea was to maintain a convenient daily record of the disposition of merchant shipping in the area. At first I applied myself enthusiastically to the placing of pins. When, after several weeks, it became clear to me that the map was never consulted, my efforts slackened; I began to bring the flags up to date not twice daily, as instructed, but at intervals of one, two, and then three days. There were even certain ships—those going to Macao or Swatow or Amoy—that sailed from Hong Kong and returned within a matter of days; and these, so far as I was concerned, never left port.

The change in attitude toward the map was the result not of indolence but of common sense. What kind of person, seeing the map not once consulted over a period of many weeks, would have diligently moved the pins twice daily? Through what delusions of self-importance could I have goaded myself to its careful maintenance? I was a reasonable person and had merely adapted my behavior to my observations.

I was placing the flags at three-day intervals when the episode of the *Van Heutz* intervened.

The *Van Heutz*, a Dutch liner cruising the Orient with war-weary Europeans, was attacked and boarded on the high seas by Chinese pirates, who seized control of the ship, sailed her to a remote bay on the China coast, and ransomed a number of the passengers, having first sifted them for valuables. When news of the drama broke on Hong Kong, a baffled group of officials was found before my map, vainly seeking some news of this ship—which had, alas, not yet qualified for my attention.

My downfall was not complete. After some days in eclipse I was rehabilitated and also allowed to chalk in red and blue crayon on a different map the daily gains and losses of the civil war.

It was the most delightful office imaginable. It was staffed largely by very young Englishmen of greatly varying personalities and backgrounds. Lanky and fair, short and swarthy, languid or dynamic, they were alike in my eyes in belonging irrefutably to the real world. They had all seen active service in the war—yet they were still so young that there was discernable in their conversation that (not always negligible) wit of the Fifth Form, which remains with many Englishmen throughout their lives. They were familiar with Homer, quoted Auden, and on their free afternoons would go down to the Dairy Farm Restaurant in Des Voeux Road and eat up platefuls of colored ice cream. Enthusiasm would have been against their principles, but there was an element of optimism in their charm; the war had ended, and I think we were all relieved simply to find ourselves alive.

When not engaged with my maps, I shared a small office with the filing clerk, a Mr. Crackenthorpe, and a Chinese translator whose given name was Tik. The filing clerk, a man of Pickwickian appearance, was known as Mr. C. He had spent his entire adult life abroad in the service of his own country, indefatigably keeping the records of international intrigue. Although he had lived in startling places for staggering stretches of time, he had in no other sense left his native land, its sounder practices and better characteristics being as strong in him as on the day he first set forth. He uttered few words of his own language and knew no word of any other. His maximum effort toward bridging the language gap was made each morning when he gave his hearty greeting in pidgin English to the pair of amahs who cleaned our offices. Astonishing expressions then fell from his lips, such as "Catchem top-side cleanee by and by," or "Wipem deskee chopchop," or that wistful and irrelevant pronouncement on the greenness of far fields, "Canton more far."

Tik, on the other hand, was fluent in various languages. He worked in both Mandarin and Cantonese, but his mother tongue was Haka, a dialect of the hill people in the coastal areas opposite Hong Kong. He was a man of great courtesy and control, never showing anger or impatience or giving the slightest sign that he was suppressing them. Between assaults on my maps, I learned from him Chinese words and phrases and the composition of certain characters—all of which I have inexcusably forgotten—but he spent most of his day bent over the documents or newspapers he was required to translate. His face struck me as perfectly matched with his name (which was pronounced "teak," like the wood), being a deep, supple sun color, glossy yet grainy, and richly polished by its encounters with the world.

I imagined all this to be typical of office life and could not understand what people were complaining about. I yearned to distinguish myself more favorably with this company, and not long after the debacle of the *Van Heutz* an opportunity presented itself.

One morning as I was faithfully populating the China Sea with my colored pins, a discussion took place in my presence—a discussion concerned with a mysterious figure and his sinister activities. Sinister acts and mysterious personages are, as is well known, a commonplace in the East, and this office of mine was in one way or another acquainted with many of them, constituting as they did the very commodity in which it dealt. The man discussed that morning—whom I will call Mr. Jarvis, for the excellent reason that that was not his true name—was distinguished from all previous cases only by the fact that I personally knew of him, having met his wife on various occasions at the Cricket Club. I would have been less than human—or older than sixteen—had I divulged this on the spot. The discussion took a gratifying turn. I was detached from the map and within a few minutes had told all I knew of the Jarvises, which was merely that they lived in Canton and frequently made the short trip to Hong Kong. I had never been to Canton, and Mrs. Jarvis, on the latest of our meetings at the Cricket Club, had invited me to stay with them there whenever I wished.

It should be remembered that my employers were very young. Within the hour I had written to the Jarvises. Within the week I was setting out for Canton. Like most sudden developments, this was less dramatic at the time than it now appears to be, for I was merely doing what I might in any case have done, and the object of my visit, though concealed, was nothing more than to observe the way in which the Jarvises lived—whom they knew and where they went. (I don't think that at the outset I thought much about this object; the true significance of the journey, as far as I was concerned, lay in being sent at all and was therefore already established.) A weekend at Canton with Cricket Club acquaintances seemed to my family to be a thoroughly acceptable diversion for me, and I myself approached the outing in something of this spirit. I do remember that I was enjoined to a deeper degree of secrecy than I had previously undertaken to observe; this was a wise precaution.

The short trip to Canton could be made by boat, train, or plane. I chose the plane, for I had never flown before and it seemed an appropriate occasion. The Jarvises undertook to meet me at the other end.

I left after lunch on a Saturday, so that I could be back at my maps on Monday morning.

The Hong Kong airfield of Kai Tak had been formed on a narrow strip of reclaimed land, on the mainland opposite Hong Kong—on the British side of the border, between the harbor and the arid mountains of South China. Of the planes that rose there in confined spirals all day long, only a few were commercial, the remainder belonging at that time to a big RAF base. The office of the airline had been set up in a Quonset hut and consisted of two or three scarred desks beleaguered by passengers and defended by the company's officials. My fellow-travelers were mostly Chinese—men going to Canton on business or to visit relatives. Some wore light cotton suits, some loose jackets and trousers, some the simple poorer suits of oiled black silk.

Through some standard injustice, I was led to the front of this crowd. The man behind the desk, a young Eurasian, at once set aside the papers he was marking and consulted another page, handwritten in English. He ticked off my name and told me I would be called. I was sent to sit down on a wooden bench at the far end of the hut, where the single other non-Chinese passenger, a young man with a newspaper, was already waiting alone.

A glance at this young man revealed him to be an American—his light hair cropped like a convict's, his loose suit worn without flair, and he was eating something. His young face had, so I complacently thought, the unfinished look of his country. When I reached the bench he looked up from his newspaper, then folded it in the middle and put it down, unaffectedly preparing to talk.

I had always been warned not to speak to strangers. I had been told, too, that Americans were a precipitate people. I sat down at the other end of the bench. The tin hut was preposterously hot. From beneath the bench came a sound of heavy panting, and a dog materialized—an unattractive dog, an old, tough, and distressingly hairless dog—and collapsed, still puffing, at our feet.

The young man spoke to me. I looked at him obliquely. He was holding something toward me in his fingers.

"No, thank you." I occupied myself with the dog. "Here, doggie." I extended my hand. The dog paid me no attention.

"Doesn't speak English," suggested the young man on the bench.

"Possibly not," I agreed remotely. "But perhaps he understands it."

The young man laughed. He brought out his cigarettes. "You smoke?"

"No," I said, unaccountably pleased.

"Going to Canton for a visit?"

"To stay with friends."

"You live in Hong Kong?"

"With my parents." (Such questions were unpardonable, but it was gratifying to be asked them.)

"Well," he remarked, looking me over, "they certainly got you up to look like Alice in Wonderland." He plucked at his own sleeve. "Sharkskin," he said.

I showed polite interest, and he went on to tell me that the suit had been made in Hong Kong in twenty-four hours. Certainly it showed no sign of prolonged attention.

The dog heaved itself nearer, and the young man nudged it good-naturedly with his foot. "You travel much on your own?"

"Oh sometimes," I replied carelessly.

"How old are you?"

"Sixteen," I said, aloof again.

"Jesus."

"What do you do?" I inquired, adapting to the questions game.

"I survey airfields," he said, "to see if we can use them." He brought out his card and gave it to me. "I've been in China six months, surveying for the company."

I was too polite to ask which company or to look at the card. "Have you liked it?" I asked instead.

"God," he said elusively. "What a place."

I nodded.

"This thing is changing so fast."

"This thing," I cautiously agreed.

"God knows what's going to happen. A couple of years from now, all this"—his gesture had no reference to the steaming hut—"will be gone. Finished."

Unexpectedly, he reminded me of my colleagues at the office. In every way their opposite, he yet conveyed something of their appeal.

He glanced up. "I guess we can go now." He picked up my little wicker suitcase.

"Oh—I can carry that."

"No reason to." In his other hand he had a heavy zipper bag of his own. We crossed the hut, and the dog followed us with incurious eyes, not lifting his head. The Chinese passengers were filing out, and we fell in line.

The plane was very confused and smelled of fumigation. "These Dakotas," said my friend. "Terrible." When he had arranged our luggage precariously in a mesh rack, he added, "This is the most dangerous airfield in the world." We seated ourselves together at the back of the plane, and he helped me to fasten the seat belt. "If there *is* a worse airfield than this," he said, "it's the one we're going to at Canton."

"What's wrong with it?" I asked fearlessly.

He grinned. "Just to give you an idea," he said. "It's called Flying Cloud."

We roared. We rushed over bumpy ground. We tilted and rose into the air. One passenger wailed; another was sick. The eroded hills came alarmingly close, then fell away. Widening valleys, improbably green, spread out from a sluggish river.

My companion gave me a peppermint for my ears. "When I get back to Hong Kong," he said, "I might look you up."

I wondered if this could be considered picking someone up.

"If you'd like that."

"I would like it," I said meekly. "Yes."

"Of course," he continued, "it may involve telling me your name."

I told him and he wrote it down—with difficulty because of the vibrations—in a small notebook, and printed "Gloucester" underneath. We were silent for some moments. I then turned to him and leaned forward to make myself heard. "As it happens," I shrieked offhandedly, "I've never actually flown before."

I never did see him again, although the following week he sent me a postcard from Taipei—which, together with the visiting card, seemed to add up to a substantial tribute. He had what I thought of as an authentic American name, with an Old Testament name and a middle initial. I remembered it for years.

The Jarvises had sent their driver to Flying Cloud, and this driver's name was Feng. Feng was small, brisk, and very talkative; he got me quickly through Chinese customs (no mean feat) and into a green Dodge. "Famous airfield," he observed, with no note of sarcasm, as we drove away from the sheds of Flying Cloud. He then explained that Mrs. Jarvis would meet us in town, and that Mr. Jarvis had been called away to Shanghai on business.

A bad road lay across flat land before us, and over this we made terrifyingly good time—I digesting the departure of Mr. Jarvis, and Feng talking a great deal. Nothing can make one feel more alien than the contours of Eastern lands, those landscapes that have never heard of Romanticism or Impressionism, that will not play the game, and that we greet as fantasy when we find them in art. The curiously separate hills with their fronded separate trees filed past us as we raced over the valley floor, in the muddy trough of the road. "Famous burial ground," said Feng, nodding to a terraced hillside, and "Famous monument," as we passed a great flight of steps. There followed in quick succession a famous wall, a famous crossroads, and an ill-famed prison before we entered the city by one of its most famous boulevards. There was Mrs. Jarvis, standing at the rim of the sidewalk, her open parasol resting on her shoulder. Feng drew the car recklessly to the gutter, braked, and leapt out to welcome me to the famous soil—which indeed formed part of the ill-paved curb onto which I stepped.

When Mrs. Jarvis had greeted me, she sent Feng elsewhere. I saw that she was considerate with him, making sure the errand would not keep him late, inquiring where he would get his dinner. When she finally turned to me, she smiled and took hold of my fingers, and we walked a little way along the congested street holding hands.

It is not possible to hold hands for long in a street such as that. (One of the most pleasant of Chinese customs is for friends, particularly a group of young people, to clasp hands as they walk along, but this is achieved by a chain effect, so that the group walks in linked file.) Mrs. Jarvis and I soon parted, but the contact was her means of making me feel welcome. I now suppose her to have been about forty-five—she was one of the anomalous ages then belonging in my mind to relatives and school-teachers. She was pale, patient, rather frail, with traces of that flat-curled, large-eyed prettiness that in my childhood was associated with Alice Faye. I do not remember her dress, and I suspect that her dresses were not memorable. She had, for an Englishwoman, a low-pitched and indecisive voice, and her general air, though passive, was one of appeal.

She had thought I might like to see the shops before we went home for tea. I dutifully took an interest in the forest of little shops, the bolts of material, the endless plastic shoes and handbags, the ivory elephants and Madonnas, the jade curios and jewelry mounted in red gold. Out of deference to Mrs. Jarvis I bought a pretty handkerchief in a linen shop; out of deference to Chinese law I paid with a huge bundle of Chinese bills (the currency having lately gotten literally out of hand) instead of with the American dollars I also had in my wicker bag, and in this I was possibly unique among travelers in China at the time.

Mrs. Jarvis hailed a pedicab. In the pedicab she put up her parasol—it was a red one of glazed papier-mâché, the kind sold by hawkers on street corners during the rainy season—and I wondered if she did this for protection from the sun or from the beggars who plaintively detained us at every turn. Once the roofs of a temple were pointed out, once a desolate park surrounding an unkempt shrine, but there was no suggestion that we should visit either. The road became less commercial and less crowded, and turned at last toward the river.

The Jarvises lived with the European community of Canton, on the island of Shameen in the Pearl River. This "island," which had long ago been formed of a mud bank reinforced with granite, lay in a bend of the river and was at one point so closely connected to the bank that the bridge there seemed to be spanning a mere moat—a token separation of East and West. The Japanese, Mrs. Jarvis informed me, had filled in the moat with earth when they occupied Canton during the war, but it had since been dug out again. By whom, I wondered, and on whose orders? It was a strange time to reactivate a moat.

Shameen was forbidden to traffic. Mrs. Jarvis and I crossed the causeway on foot and walked down a shaded road, past sober Western buildings, none large but all substantial. I remember the silence, the freshness of the trees after the squalid streets we had just come through, and the immediate sense of boredom—for here once more was the enclosed colonial life, in this case divided by a moat from the uproar of reality. Perhaps it is too much to say that this atmosphere was only emphasized by the fact that the British Consulate had recently been burned. It had been burned, not as a manifestation of universal change but in what might be called the old spirit—as a reprisal for a local incident involving disputed territory near Hong Kong. Roofless, its gray façade still stood, mounted on wide steps and surmounted by a charred "*Honi soit* . . . " The incident, in retrospect, has the antiquated air of a self-contained protest that had little reference to the world in general.

Mrs. Jarvis's apartment was on the third floor of a small compound, and looked onto a courtyard of trees. A houseboy let us in, but there was no sound within the house and little light. Hot sunshine came dimly through rattan blinds. Ceiling fans revolved in every room.

A narrow bed had been made up for me in Mrs. Jarvis's own bedroom; it was, she explained, the coolest room in the flat. A mosquito net was looped above her double bed. At the far side of the bed, on a night table, lay a pipe and a copy of *Forever Amber*. These were the first—and last—details I ever learned about the person of Mr. Jarvis.

The living room, where we had tea, had been densely furnished with camphor chests and with blackwood chairs and tables, among which a jagged incision had been made by means of a folding screen. The walls were covered with photographs, and the floor with mats of some glossy reed. The room opened into a second salon, more gloomy than the first, where the dark outline of a grand piano could be dimly seen, sailing without lights like a ship at war.

Mrs. Jarvis brought photographs over to the tea table and identified them. This was Jeremy, shown here in his flight sergeant's uniform but now in a London bank; that was Philip, studying to be an engineer; and here was Janice in color, a rosy version of her mother, charming beneath her nurse's cap.

To the casual observation that she must miss them, Mrs. Jarvis responded with silence and a motion of the head that shook back tears.

The evening, like the afternoon, was an oddly domestic one to offer a visitor in a strange and ancient city. We passed it sitting by the screened windows when the blinds had been drawn up to let in the dusk, Mrs. Jarvis writing letters and I reading *Rebecca*, which I had found in a bookcase. I was struck by the loneliness of Mrs. Jarvis's life. Was it different when Mr. Jarvis was there? Did this gloomy drawing room ever resound to the hearty (or even sinister) laughter of cronies? Was it ever fully lit of occupied? One somehow felt not.

Mrs. Jarvis kept early hours. It was strange to be going to sleep at ten o'clock in the very heart of that most sleepless of cities, stranger still to be camped, as it were, in this immaculate clearing of a man-made jungle. While the city fought for its jostling, noisy, desperate existence, Mrs. Jarvis and I sat up in our white beds reading, the fan turned off lest we catch—unlikely word—cold, a thermos of boiled water beside each of our beds. Before putting out the light, Mrs. Jarvis got up and adjusted her mosquito net so that it fell right around the bed. She put lotion on her lands. She did not say she was glad to have me there or that I reminded her of Janice, both these things being apparent. She merely kissed me and climbed back beneath her stifling tent.

My situation, as I look back on it, seems quite extraordinary, but at the time I found it less so. At the age of sixteen one expects almost anything of life, including much more straightforward drama than is likely to materialize; for all I knew, the position in which I found myself, if not commonplace, was a fair sample of what one might reasonably expect. It would please me to be able to say, in retrospect, that I had begun to feel repugnance for the object of my visit, but I think this was not the case. I was not an unduly callous child, but scruples of this sort develop against the background of experience and are not, I imagine, commonly found in adolescents in a spontaneous form. Mrs. Jarvis was a parent—that is to say she was of parental age and aspect, and that her touchingly maternal attitude toward me (illustrated even by the presence of my bed in her room) confirmed her in this role; I was still at an age that views almost any deception of a parent as not only permissible but even essential to mutual survival. Above all, I was conditioned by a wartime childhood to think of such missions as mine in terms not of violation and duplicity but of honor and even valor.

I make these points not to excuse myself but to explain what follows in its true light—as it really was, an insight into my own character. As I lay that night in Canton in my hot little bed it became perfectly obvious to me that, whatever revelations there might be concerning the Jarvis household, I was not the one to make them; that whatever astute question might bring forth an avalanche of significant detail, I was not the one to ask it; that I had no aptitude for such a task, and that were I to remain a week, a fortnight, a month in the Jarvis ménage, I would be none the wiser. This discovery about myself, far from bringing any satisfaction, was dark with the sense of failure. My desire to accomplish my mission and ingratiate myself with my superiors was very great; the prospect of returning empty-handed cast a pall of desperation over the whole experience. It now seemed to be repeating, in some way I could not determine, the characteristics of the *Van Heutz* affair—in which I had displayed an inability to consider all the possibilities. Wondering what the missing possibilities might be in this case, I fell asleep.

The following morning I sat on the living-room floor and read *Rebecca*. The weather, very usual for the time of year, was an alternation of glowering sunshine and sudden downpour that sent up a steamy odor of vegetation from the garden. The Jarvis's apartment had its own contrasting smell—a shuttered smell of mildew and insect spray, of furniture polish and face powder, the smell of colonial houses in the Orient. There was about this, as about the apartment in general, something so true to form, so representative of the British community, as practically to exonerate the Jarvises there and then from any suggestion of foul play. Someone operating against his country's interests would, one imagined, hardly have found it possible to align himself so uncompromisingly with its attributes—might even have introduced a note of interest, some telltale innovation of taste or atmosphere. Such conditions as those in which the Jarvises lived could not be reproduced by contrivance; their most outstanding feature was their complete lack of premeditation.

In the afternoon we took the ferry some distance up the river to visit friends of Mrs. Jarvis. "They are Germans," she told me. By this time I was sunk into a despondency from which not even the promising word "Germans" could rouse me, and when she added "Missionaries," it was no more than I expected.

The Pearl River, which at Canton is approaching its estuary, is of a precariously alluvial color and a consistency sometimes closer to that of flowing land than water. Before it reaches the sea, the river must in fact pass through a narrow, steeply banked channel, but here at Canton one can easily imagine that it has completed its course and that the ocean is at hand, so great is the sense of a harbor. On this illusory harbor, dense suburbs of sampans rose and fell with the river, so thickly gathered that they seemed to be swarming ashore and to have mingled with the dun-colored habitations on land. Families had even made temporary settlements on the rafts formed by logs moored at the docks of timberlands. Our ferry, a game and grimy little affair, kept to a central channel more or less cleared for river traffic, and soon left all this behind.

Mrs. Jarvis's friends lived within sight of the river, in a straggling, almost rural suburb. They were a white-haired couple, simple, resigned, and kind, who had spent most of their lives in China. They talked of change, and of what it had been like to live in Canton throughout the Japanese occupation (during which they had, embarrassingly, not been interned like the rest of one's European acquaintance). Their house was set in a curious little plot of land, almost a farm, where there were vegetable gardens, a chicken coop, and a small orchard. The house itself was wooden and rather run-down; the porch on which we sat had a frieze of wooden fretwork and was floored by uneven boards, long unpainted. The place had an inconsequential, forgotten air, like the provincial setting of a Russian novel, so that one's eyes constantly wandered toward the river for confirmation of one's own existence. After tea, the old man fell asleep in his chair. We took our leave in whispers, and the ferry carried us back to Shameen.

In the end, I suppose, the prolonged hush of the weekend got the better of me. Or possibly, since I had come to Canton for revelations and no one else had provided them, I felt an urge to do so myself. That evening, when Mrs. Jarvis and I sat down by the windows, I talked a great deal. Her very reticence invited confidences, a vacuum to be filled, and I told her about my attachments and amusements—whom I knew, in fact, and where I went. I think I even told her about my school days. That is stopped short of enlightening her about my presence in her house may have been due to good luck rather than discretion—for although she was a sympathetic listener, she saw no reason to postpone her bedtime. As on the previous evening, we were in bed by ten.

It was Feng who took me to the plane the following morning. Mrs. Jarvis and I said goodbye to one another at the Shameen causeway. We promised to be in touch soon, and she gave me *Rebecca* to read on the plane. She asked Feng to take good care of me—which, after his fashion, he did, driving me frantically to the airport and seeing me safely on board the famous plane.

I did not see Mrs. Jarvis again, although we exchanged a letter or two, for the Jarvises moved to Manila a few months later, taking with them their blackwood and camphor trappings from Canton. Perhaps they are living there still.

My employers showed understanding about my lack of success. Perhaps their expectations had not been great, or they were relieved that I had not proved troublesome. In any event, after the first report, no inquiries were made of me and I was allowed to go on with my war-map in peace. I did not, of course, say that I had failed; I tried to convey a sense of mystery.

PAPYROLOGY AT NAPLES

Over thirty years ago, the Italian poet Eugenio Montale hoped—unavailingly, as he knew—for at least one Italian city of silence, which, immune to the profitable hubbub of current attractions, would allow visitors serene contemplation of its beauty and antiquity. Naples is far from silent. Yet the city's apparent unconcern with tourism is possibly part of a larger Neapolitan indifference to processed "event" as contrasted with distinct occasion. When it chooses, Naples can meet an occasion in resplendent style. And at such moments it is as though in a moldering theatre a curtain rises on a solemn and beautiful scene whose actors move with complete assurance and whose charm and majesty pervade the audience itself. It was in this spirit that Naples, last spring, gave hospitality in a series of historical settings to a gathering peculiarly congenial to the city's temperament and story.

A novice attending the Seventeenth International Congress of Papyrology during that alternately hot and stormy week of May might not have expected to find in the five hundred participants the animated and generally youthful assembly—of men and women in almost equal numbers—who discoursed on themes derived from the ancient writings that form their life study. Their discussions ranged from the most consequential events of the ancient world to the humblest details of its daily life: from Homeric texts to the salt tax; from the epigrams of imperial Rome to the composition of a remote Roman garrison; from the price of slaves in the second century before Christ to the installation of Egyptian bishops five centuries later; from ancient musical notation to the tax exemption enjoyed by acolytes of the crocodile god. The names of Plato and Epicurus, of Simonides and Menander, of William Hamilton and Joseph Banks were familiarly invoked as speakers moved from one chosen millennium to another.

Presentations were brief and intense; questions in themselves revealing. (A number omitted from an arithmetic lesson by a forgetful schoolchild of ancient Egypt drew the inquiry "Was the number in Roman or in Ptolemaic?" and the response "In Ptolemaic.") A Greek text in Latin characters, or a Latin text in Greek, posed special difficulties, as did the dating of *ostraca*. Formidable erudition was imparted with an amiability whose very disclaimers were stylish ("I am not myself a demoticist"). Papyrologists from virtually all countries of Western Europe, and from the Middle East and the United States, delivered talks, without interpretation, in Italian, English, German, or French. A sprinkling of other participants had travelled from Canada, from Australia, from Argentina to present their papers. The presence of East European and Soviet scholars (whose expenses, in case of need, are guaranteed through the International Association of Papyrologists for attendance at these triennial meetings) was apparently precluded by their governments, in pursuance of a recurrent pattern; and this offense against humanity and scholarship was formally deplored by the congress in its closing motions.

Papyrology—a word that, taken literally, would refer to the medium rather than the message—properly designates the study of papyri written in Greek or Latin, papyri in Egyptian script being considered a branch of Egyptology. The vast preponderance of extant classical papyri derive from Egypt—and are in Greek, since Greek remained the lingua franca of the eastern Mediterranean from the time of Alexander the Great until the close of the Roman Empire. Throughout that period of a thousand years, immense quantities of papyrus shipped from Egypt, where the material was exclusively produced, supplied the needs of Europe. (As late as the seventh century, according to a surviving document, Egyptian papyrus was being procured by Frankish Gaul.) The manufacture of rag paper, long practiced in China and conveyed by the Arabs to the Western world, became usual in Europe only in the Middle Ages.

Use of the papyrus reed by the ancient Egyptian, Greek, and Roman civilizations as a device for receiving and retaining script so proliferated as to leave, in that resistant medium, a multitude of surviving documents. In the age of the Antonines, as Gibbon tells us, "Homer as well as Virgil were transcribed and studied on the banks of the Rhine and Danube,"[1] and the literary legacy was accompanied by detailed records of empires, communities, and individual lives. Failure of the Egyptian papyrus crop could mean to the Roman world a paralysis of commerce and affairs of state, and suspension of work for innumerable scribes who carried on the enormous labor of transcription. Many of the scribes were, like the father of the Emperor Diocletian, literate slaves; while the cultivated members of Roman society commemorated literacy, as had the Egyptians before them, by occasionally displaying in portraits their diverse writing materials—which, in addition to papyrus, included parchment, wax tablets, and board. (In the fifth century, St. Augustine felt obliged to apologize to a correspondent for a letter written on vellum rather than papyrus.[2])

The huge deposits of Greek papyri recovered in Egypt during the late nineteenth century by foreign archeologists and clandestine local diggers dramatically extended the scope and nature of papyrology, and transformed the study of ancient history. Significant new discoveries of ancient writings—such as the leathern Dead Sea Scrolls, or the first surviving complete play by Greek poet Menander (who, by a pleasing irony, appears in a frescoed depiction at Pompeii, manuscript in hand)—continue to fire the public as well as the scholarly imagination, for written evidence from the human past exerts human fascination. In this regard, as with much else at Naples, the city's associations are peculiarly dramatic—from the narrow survival of Virgil's epic exaltation of the Neapolitan ambience to the systematic burning by the Germans in the Second World War of capital portions of the city's ancient archive. Through more than twenty centuries of Neapolitan turmoil, the greatest writers have emerged to report the city's story with thrilling immediacy. The contemporary historian Roberto Pane (himself, at eighty-six, a Neapolitan legend) once drew my attention to a curious literary "pairing" of two cataclysmic events at Naples described in celebrated letters by two men of genius—the great eruption of Vesuvius in 79 AD, recounted to Tacitus by the younger Pliny; and the destruction of the port of Naples in the deluge of 1343, magnificently related by Petrarch, within hours of the occurrence, in a letter to his friend Cardinal Giovanni Colonna.

In one respect beyond all others, however, the choice of Naples as the site of the 1983 Congress of Papyrology had intense and excruciating meaning. For that antique city possesses, at the foot of its presiding volcano, a buried repository of ancient documents, broached two centuries ago and subsequently resealed. In 1750, during initial excavations of the Roman towns engulfed in the eruption of 79 AD, the so-called Villa dei Papiri was discovered—an opulent private establishment near Herculaneum containing, together with splendid works of ancient sculpture in marble and bronze, a collection of scrolled Greek and Latin texts denoting an important library. Approached by a process of tunneling from the foot of a shaft twenty-seven meters deep, this Roman villa was only partly penetrated before exhalations of volcanic gas compelled the excavators to close all access to it, in 1765. Statues and decoration removed from the excavation—and today on view at the National Archaeological Museum in Naples—contributed to the neoclassical impact on Western taste and knowledge produced by the great Vesuvian discoveries at Herculaneum and Pompeii, and at other sites under the volcano. The inscribed scrolls—now catalogued as nearly two thousand items—removed from the library required more perseverance. Carbonized in their long seclusion, they at first defied attempts to unroll them, yielding only to a painstaking technique after dozens had been fatally mangled. The first work to be deciphered—Philodemus's treatise on music—was gradually followed by discoveries of a philosophical and literary nature, notably on the Epicurean concepts informing Roman thought and society. The scrolls are now conserved, many of them still inexorably furled, in the National Library at Naples.

"One hates writing descriptions that are to be found in every book of travels; but we have seen something today that I am sure you never read of, and perhaps never heard of." Thus, in June of 1740, Horace Walpole, on the Grand Tour, began his splendid letter describing these first revelations at Herculaneum, where excavations had only recently commenced. "There might certainly be collected great light from this reservoir of antiquities," he concluded, "if a man of learning had the inspection of it.[3] Since 1765, no sustained effort has been made to excavate the Villa dei Papiri, although scholars and poets have continually appealed against its abandoned state. By 1835, Giacomo Leopardi, who was to spend some of his last months of life at a house close to Herculaneum, was calling down "eternal shame and vituperation" on Italy's neglect of the buried documents.[4] And Norman Douglas, commenting seventy years ago on the incalculable importance of the villa's unretrieved library, pessimistically observed that "whoever wishes to consult it must wait till a generation which really possesses the civilization it vaunts, shall rescue it from the lava of Herculaneum."[5] Not everyone is prepared to accept such lasting, or everlasting, postponement. At a meeting held at the eighteenth-century Villa Campolieto, near Herculaneum, the 1983 papyrology congress emphatically urged reexcavation. Advanced techniques not only in archaeology but also in the treatment of papyrus (by enzymes, for example) are now available for a task made urgent by deterioration of the treasure underground—and by the imponderable energies of the fateful mountain above.

Informed voices and devoted efforts have not been lacking, at Naples and elsewhere, in support of renewing the excavation; and in recent years a feasibility study was planned, during a transient show of Italian governmental interest. However, following the construction, close to the villa's site, of an expensive, uncompleted "antiquarium" of grim aspect and dubious utility, the project seems to have lapsed. The Italian government's neglect of inestimable riches in the immediate vicinity—in much of Pompeii, for example, and in the decaying group of eighteenth-century "Vesuvian villas," among which Vanvitelli's Campolieto offers a quite unwonted instance of restoration—and the encroachment of new suburbs at Herculaneum itself give small confidence for a show of official sanity toward the Villa dei Papiri.

In the nineteen eighties, it is not difficult to discern in all this a parable for an era that, gazing into outer space, cannot look inward. In fact, the ancient cities of Vesuvius have served as object lessons from the very moments of their destruction, when an unknown hand, presumed to be that of a Jew or an early Christian, scrawled "Sodom Gomor" on a Pompeian wall—a curiosity that was to capture the imagination of Proust. During last May's congress, a Neapolitan participant, Carlo Knight, observed that the symbolic drama of the Villa dei Papiri seems unending: "Two thousand years after the tragedy, Herculaneum is still an incurable wound."

While the Villa dei Papiri remains an underground enigma by the Mediterranean, a curious monument to it has been raised in the New World. The decision of the late J. Paul Getty, in constructing his museum at Malibu in the early nineteen seventies, to "re-create"—as he expressed it—the Villa dei Papiri of Herculaneum was heard with wonder at Naples. Conjecture about the original villa's appearance is based on the calculations of a Swiss engineer named Karl Weber, who, in directing the early excavations, established the floor plan of the ample structure, which covered an area of approximately 250 by a 140 meters. While the elaborate, costly, and somewhat bizarre construction at Malibu does not claim to adhere consistently to our fragmentary knowledge of the original building, it incorporates, on the same grand scale, the peristyle gardens and colonnaded views toward the sea, and employs the felicitous Roman combination of graceful planting and ornamental water works known to have enhanced the Villa dei Papiri.

Among the beautiful collections of the Getty Museum are just such antiquities as those that adorned the ancient cities of Vesuvius. And, during his own repeated visits to Naples, J. Paul Getty showed particular interest in the excavations at Herculaneum and its neighboring classical sites. It was therefore natural that eyes should turn from Naples to Malibu in hope of assistance in rescuing the Getty's great precursor and its entombed treasure. As yet, they have turned in vain. In 1974, to an appeal of the kind from Neapolitan authorities, Mr. Getty replied, "My charitable budget is fully committed." He proposed the 17 million dollars spent on his Malibu reconstruction as sufficient recognition of Herculaneum's importance, and expressed the hope that "others may be inspired by my example." The terms of the Getty trust apparently do not exclude future consideration of—in the words of one Getty administrator—"activities in various parts of the world that would be consistent with these commitments." For the present, however, the title of the Getty's publication on its architectural genesis, "From Herculaneum to Malibu," appears to suggest the direction in which Getty is flowing.[6]

As a body, papyrologists seem slow to wrath, and the Getty Museum's decision not to send a representative to this spring's congress at Naples was philosophically received. It may be that the profession accustoms its practitioners to the immemorial vagaries of mankind. In our time, papyrologists have been forced to flee their European universities for sanctuary in other lands, bearing their knowledge with them like a faith, while American papyrologists of the older generation—exemplified at the Naples congress by Naphtali Lewis, distinguished professor emeritus of the City University of New York—have seen their profession burgeon in the United States from sparse beginnings into a discipline now comparable, in quality if not yet in magnitude, to its European counterparts.

The concept of written language was not common to all ancient cultures, and trends of our own era indicate how it might die out or revert, as in past ages, to a skill practiced by an accomplished few. In such a context, every gesture of civilized meaning gives courage. As the Naples congress closed, its organizing spirit, Professor Marcello Gigante, director of the Institute of Classical Philology at the University of Naples, described it as "*un atto di amore*" on the part of Naples toward culture. His words might be understood as a *coronis*, that is, as the little flourish of penmanship with which the scribes of other times concluded their patient scrolls.

THE TUSCAN IN EACH OF US

The anthem of praise raised by foreign writers—and in particular by writers in English—to Italy, to Tuscany, to Florence, has consistently sounded a note of relief. Its theme is that of a heaven-sent rescue: the rescue of the self from incompleteness. We realize that we had always dreamed we might dwell among such scenes and sentiments, and now we find our wish consummated. We celebrate an environment that is both a revelation and a repose to us, a consolation and a home. Like all love, this love of foreigners for Tuscany is easy to mock. Like all love, it is an object of envy on the part of those who feel excluded from it. (And let us remember the observation of Dr. Johnson: "A man who has not been in Italy is always conscious of an inferiority."[1]) We are told that it is not original, it is not realistic. It is true that there may be illusion in it, and a lack of what is currently defined as realism. But does it not seem to you, in these times, that in the name of realism we are being asked to mock our very souls?

Illusion is part of civilized power. Wherever there is civilization, there is to some degree illusion. Yeats says that

> Civilization is hooped together, brought
> Under a rule, under the semblance of peace
> By manifold illusion.[2]

And Clough, in his beautiful poem, *Amours de Voyage*, reflects on Italy:

> Is it illusion or not that attracteth the pilgrim transalpine
> Brings him a dullard and dunce hither to pry and to stare?
> Is it illusion or not that allures the barbarian stranger,
> Brings him with gold to the shrine, brings him in arms to the gate?[3]

As E. M. Forster's hero Fielding arrives in Italy from the Orient, Forster tells us that "a cup of beauty was lifted to his lips, and he drank with a sense of disloyalty. . . . He had forgotten the beauty of form . . . the harmony between the works of man and the earth that upholds them. . . . The Mediterranean"—says Forster—"is the human norm. When men leave that exquisite lake, whether through the Bosphorous or the Pillars of Hercules, they approach the monstrous and extraordinary."[4]

The Mediterranean, as an ideal, is the human norm. Not a norm as a leveling, nor as *la legge della media*, but an equilibrium in which individual quality can rationally flourish. Comprehensiveness here, and comprehension, have time and again restored our disparate elements to form and healed us.

Winckelmann spoke for many of us when he said that "God owed me Italy, for I had suffered too much in my youth."[5] Release, expansiveness, the nurturing of elements intrinsic but denied—these are the themes even of such a rigorous observer as D. H. Lawrence. We embrace this culture as our own, in the beautiful phrase of Burchardt, "by a kind of hereditary right or by right of admiration"—not so much undergoing a transformation as acknowledging at last the Tuscan in each of us.[6]

That sense of rightfulness has its definable source in humanism. Outsiders have been drawn to Tuscany and to Florence as to the center and capital of their own civilized values. One might almost say that even those—and they are many—who come to Florence to buy new shoes and table linen do so, in some remote degree, in the name of humanism: for they have heard that Florence matters. Travelers from lands where humanism is unknown respond to the Tuscan phenomenon, and perhaps this refers to the humanist in each of us. In the newer societies beyond these shores I believe that we begin to see the death of humanism; and this is even urged on in the name of that unexamined "reality" and in unchallenged retreat from individualism although none can predict what loss of humanistic values will mean, or what will be the future moral bearing of humanity. These matters already have their strong effects on Tuscan life, but here we are nevertheless made aware that what was so many centuries in the making will not surrender easily. In fact, that sensation of relief that Tuscany has always afforded to outsiders has been recharged in recent years: for here, as yet, humanism labors under no disfavor and need not appear self-conscious. Like Machiavelli in his great letter from S. Andrea in Percussina, we shed here much nonsense unworthy of our better selves.[7]

An Australian of my generation grew up in raw ignorance of humanism, of the Renaissance, of Tuscan art. The themes of Italy were little developed in the Australian literature that came to our hands; and although we encountered it in literature more generally, our own circumstances and those of the globe before and during the Second World War made Italy remote from us. We were given no inkling that the immemorial influences of this land had helped to form the Australian social order, and—to speak generally—Australians of those years were often inaccessible to unfamiliar concepts, and hostile to aesthetic revelation. It is notable that these Tuscan places that played so prominent a part in English and European literature figure only exceptionally in Australian writing of past generations. Even now, I think of rather a few strong examples, but rather of passing incidents. In Patrick White's *Riders in the Chariot*, well-to-do Australians are glimpsed in Florence at the turn of the century, in a sarcastic aside drawn from the diary of an unhappy matron: "Norbert indefatigable. Italy his spiritual home. Only a few nights ago he embarked on a long poem on the theme of Fra Angelico. . . . Now that we are in a villa of our own, hope to discover some respectable woman who will know how to prepare him his mutton chop."[8] And in the same novel an English girl writes from Florence to her estranged suitor in England in what the author tells us is a "somewhat literary strain, about the little green hills of Tuscany, with their exciting undertones of sensuous brown," and we are informed that the recipient of the letter "had no inclination to read any farther."[9] Fortunately, perhaps, I had not read those lines when I first came to Tuscany and quite possibly wrote letters of a literary taint about its green hills—*colline, infatti, di un verdolino luminoso. Sì, centavo anch'io, come tanti altri, le giornate radiose, I campi curati come un giardino, e I solchi disegnati a calligrafia. E più di tutti parlavo—sempre" in somewhat literary strain"—delle gentilezze incredibili di questo popolo.* I lived in Siena in a scene described by a Tuscan poet—Folgore da San Gimignano—looking toward

Una montagnetta
coverta di bellissimi arboscelli,
con trenta ville e dodici castelli
che siano entorno ad una cittadetta . . . [10]

I too, like so many others before me, sat outdoors in what Leopardi calls the "sovrumani silenzi"[11] in the Tuscan night under the moon, to hear the *gufo* in the cypresses; and woke on brilliant mornings to hear the farmer shouting to the two white beasts that drew the plow. That was another Tuscany, then—though not in time historically remote. The paired white cows that pulled the plow, the close lines of vines beneath the olives, the appearance everywhere of order without uniformity or excessive regularity. For the most part, then, Tuscany was a countryside of appropriate and long-established rural buildings. One drove from Florence to Siena on the Cassia, and those two hours seemed well spent. Or once in a while by the Via Chiantigiana, which took pleasantly longer. I was too knowing to speak of Tuscany as my spiritual home, but felt it to be so. And, although I never attempted "a long poem on the theme of Fra Angelico," it was in Tuscany that I became a writer.

I have seen Florence under many conditions and have known this city in dark as well as golden days. I remember a beautiful June morning, just after daybreak, when, arriving overnight by train from Geneva, I crossed from the station to have my coffee at the Caffè Italia, where a waiter was hosing down the pavement. And I sat there, lacking nothing, in a state of perfect happiness I've never forgotten, realizing I was again in Tuscany. I remember too, years later, another arrival by train—this time on a December evening in 1966, when for a last freezing hour the train labored through the mud-laden flood. In those drastic weeks Florence lay as if stranded along the Arno; one looked upstream through the skeleton of the Ponte Vecchio; the familiar street ewer-befouled water-courses; and everywhere, indoors and out, the ghastly line was streaked along saturated walls. I remember, in streets and shops, the tears and courage, and the Florentine durability—the Florentine toughness. I saw the great Cimabue laid like a living casualty on a trestle-table, and the books heaped up like pulp at the Certosa di Galluzo. I saw a cat called Gianna who saved herself by clinging for a week to a ham suspended from the ceiling of a salumeria in Borgo Ognissanti. I remember that the cold was bitterest in Gavinana and San Frediano, where recovery was slowest, and in the poorer streets near Santa Croce. And I remember the hippies in their hundreds, digging out mud and sewage, sleeping on damp floors, and sitting down to eat in long rows at improvised tables. I recall the experts and museum curators, the art historians who converged on the city from Europe and America and raised funds abroad for restoration—funds that came from all around the globe; for the world was moved, and so was the Tuscan in each of us.

It is said to be a misfortune to be granted one's dearest wish. How many of us, nevertheless—outsiders like myself, achieving our desire to inhabit this peninsula—have been rewarded beyond our dreams. Because beyond dreams there is life itself and the intensity of being. Tuscany has a wealth of healing properties, but Tuscany is not a *casa di cura*. It is not a tame place but a stimulus: in the truest sense, one of the world's great powers. I think of Shelley at Florence in 1819 walking one day along the Arno to the Cascine in a hard west wind and coming home to write an immortal poem. Of that "Ode to the West Wind" he would note: "This poem was conceived and chiefly written in a wood that skirts the Arno . . . on a day when that tempestuous wind, whose temperature is at once mild and animating, was collecting the vapors which pour down the autumnal rains. They began, as I foresaw, at sunset with a violent tempest of hail and rain, attended by that magnificent thunder and lightning peculiar to the Cisalpine regions."[12]

This lovely place, in its endless richness and hospitality, has touched many great and lesser minds to emulation in the noblest meaning of the word. It has touched the Antipodes, and Australians who have never visited Tuscany have known it by influence and in imagination. It has moved us to do our best.

PART V

Last Words

2003 NATIONAL BOOK AWARD ACCEPTANCE

There's a moment to say I am delighted, and I am delighted. I'm delighted to have been in the company of the other nominees tonight who of recent days I've heard read from their works and been so impressed by the variety of our feelings and our approaches. There was no uniformity at all in what we brought except the wish to do well by the English language, to find the word that mattered. I honor the people who were with me because I enjoyed so much hearing them read and hearing this large diversity.

I want to say in response to Stephen King that I do not—as I think he a little bit seems to do—regard literature (which he spoke of perhaps in a slightly pejorative way), that is, the novel, poetry, language as written, I don't regard it as a competition. It is so vast. We have this marvelous language. We are so lucky that we have a huge audience for that language. If we were writing in high Norwegian, we would be writing in a great ancient language, but we would have mostly reindeer for our readers. I'm not sure that that is the ideal outcome. We have this huge language so diverse around the earth that I don't think giving us a reading list of those who are most read at this moment is much of a satisfaction because we are reading in all the ages, which have been an immense inspiration and love to me and are such an excitement.

I can take one of the ancient poems of our language and feel so excited and moved and even sometimes terrified by it that it seems very immediate to me. I don't see this as "we should read this or we should read that." We have mysterious inclinations. We have our own intuitions, our individuality toward what we want to read, and we developed that from childhood. We don't know why. Nobody can explain it to us.

I think America, especially, is drowning in explanations, and what we need is more questions, not explanations, perhaps because the explanations are not leading us into good places, at least the official ones that I hear.

I'm so grateful for readers, for writers. We are here because we love our language. We are reading and writing from both sides. It draws up all our humanity, and we need our humanity and we need our individuality, our originality. We need them more than we ever did because we are in such a position of power. I don't mean readers and writers, I mean, in this nation. We should do our best by the language. We mustn't torture it; we mustn't diminish it. We have to love it, nurture it, and enjoy it.

Pleasure, that's what we want from it, the true pleasure. A lot of information comes through pleasure and generosity, and that's what we have in literature. That's what we have in fiction.

I thank you so much for this award. It's lovely for me, but I honor every writer who is here and every reader. Thank you.

THE NEW YORK SOCIETY LIBRARY DISCUSSION, SEPTEMBER 2012

I feel very much—I have felt increasingly in recent years—that the world has a kind of Vesuvius element now, that we're waiting for something terrible to happen, and we do have an idea what it might be like, but maybe we're pleasing ourselves with that because it might be much more terrifying. And I don't want to say this to be doom-laden, but the world is not thinking—if it ever was—it's not thinking of itself as something going on forever, our world, our so-called civilized world, the world *we* live in. I think that there is now a feeling of some terrible (how shall I say), culmination that's happening, and we aren't handling this is in any (I don't mean we ourselves) way to absolutely reject that feeling; people who are sensitive to this aren't grappling with it but sort of feeling that it's almost become impossible to contest these things.

I hope I'm wrong about the doom part of this, but living in Naples, living in those ancient places, it does give you a feeling of a world that has gone on, with its errors and its triumphs and its art and its disasters, a world that's gone on like this; that there was some price to pay, ultimately. And I'm sorry to talk like this, but I think that we haven't dealt with this—I don't mean me and I don't mean you—but human beings have been living more in the immediate life and living in consumerism. And of course, scientists take much greater interest, but we aren't prepared for what is the unknown for our coming world.

We have so much good that human beings have created in our world, our literature and art, these things that many people don't participate in, but they would not have the life they have unless such things did exist in the world. And now there is, I feel, a kind of suspension: So what comes next? We know that this is leading to a world, which I hope may be better, but in which we don't understand what's happening.

NOTES

INTRODUCTION: SHIRLEY HAZZARD—AUTHOR, AMATEUR, INTELLECTUAL

1. While there is as yet no biography of Shirley Hazzard, the story of her early life is covered in the following biographical essays: Lacey Crawford, "Shirley Hazzard: A Profile," *Narrative* (Spring 2010), available at http://www.narrativemagazine.com/issues/spring-2010/shirley-hazzard; and Jan McGuinness, "The Transit of Shirley Hazzard," in *Shirley Hazzard: New Critical Essays*, ed. Brigitta Olubas (Sydney: Sydney University Press, 2014), 123–135.

2. Martin Stannard covers the matter of Hazzard's close association with key New York Intellectual figures, in particular Lionel Trilling's biography of Hazzard's close friend, Muriel Spark, in *Muriel Spark: The Biography* (London: Weidenfeld and Nicholson, 2009). In Brigitta Olubas, *Shirley Hazzard: Literary Expatriate and Cosmopolitan Humanist*, chap. 2 (Amherst, NY: Cambria Press, 2012), I consider some of the shared conceptual, political, and philosophical aspects of Hazzard's work and that of Trilling, Alfred Kazin, and Dwight MacDonald (who were also friends of Hazzard and Steegmuller), and the broader currents of liberal thought through the period.

3. Quoted in Alexander Bloom, *Prodigal Sons: The New York Intellectuals and Their World* (New York: Oxford University Press, 1986), 5.

4. Terry A. Cooney, *The Rise of the New York Intellectuals: "Partisan Review" and Its Circle* (Madison: University of Wisconsin Press, 1986), 6.

5. Richard Howard, "Fond Memory," in *Literary Lives: The World of Francis Steegmuller and Shirley Hazzard*, ed. Mark Bartlett et al. (New York: New York Society Library, 2010), 31.

6. Wendy Smith, "Shirley Hazzard: Interview," *Publishers Weekly* 23, no.10 (1990): 48–49. I provide an extended discussion of this question in Olubas, *Literary Expatriate*, chap. 2.

7. Bloom, *Prodigal Sons*, 6; Nicholas Birns, *Theory After Theory: An Intellectual History of Literary Theory from 1950 to the Early Twenty-First Century* (Buffalo, NY: Broadview Press, 2010), 18.

8. Mark Mazower, *Governing the World: The History of an Idea* (New York: Penguin, 2012), 309. For an account of Hazzard's critique of the UN as aligning with Left politics, see Nicholas Birns, "Does Idealism Preclude Heroism? Shirley Hazzard's United Nations Writings," in Olubas, *Hazzard: Essays*, 111–120.

9. Andreea Deciu Ritivoi, *Intimate Strangers: Arendt, Marcuse, Solzhenitsyn, and Said in American Political Discourse* (New York: Columbia University Press, 2014), 7.

10. See, esp., Shirley Hazzard, "A Jaded Muse," in *From Parnassus: Essays In Honor of Jacques Barzun*, ed. Dora B. Weiner and William R. Keylor (New York: Harper and Row, 1976), 121–134.

11. Shirley Hazzard, *Greene on Capri: A Memoir* (London: Virago, 2000), 9.

12. Hazzard's claims about Waldheim are included in "The League of Frightened Men," included here. Hazzard's archive contains evidence of the response to this essay. The allegation was pursued at the time by US Congressman Stephen Solarz (see Letter, Solarz to Waldheim, November 26, 1980, and reply, Waldheim to Solarz, December 19, 1980). At this point Hazzard had correspondence with a member of the Brooklyn Council, Susan D. Alter, who pursued the matter on behalf of her constituents and who confirmed Hazzard's disclosure (Letters, Alter to Hazzard, October 24, 1980, and January 2, 1981). When the story was taken up again and published by the *New Republic* writer Jane Kramer in 1986, Hazzard's role was acknowledged (Letter, Kramer to Hazzard, October 9, 1986, and reply, Hazzard to Kramer, November 6, 1986). Further evidence of the response to Hazzard's revelations can be seen in the letter from Robert Ratner, president of the UN Association to the *New Republic* (January 21, 1980) in correspondence with her friend Graham Greene (Letter, Greene to Hazzard, January 17, 1981) and in the 1980 *Washington Post* interview with Waldheim's wife that reports: "His wife is angered the most by the unsubstantiated report in Hazzard's article that Waldheim took part in the Nazi youth movement. 'That is absolutely untrue!'" (Myra McPherson, "Waldheim: The UN's Muted Peacekeeper Amid the Passion," *Washington Post*, January 18, 1980, B1, B6). After publication of Kramer's article, Solarz then pursued the matter with Waldheim (Letter, Solarz to Waldheim, April 1, 1986, and reply, Waldheim to Solarz, April 21, 1986). Copies of these letters are held in Shirley Hazzard Papers, Rare Book and Manuscript Library, Columbia University.

13. Hazzard writes in a letter to Phillip C. Jessup, former US delegate to the UN: "Lest you continue under the misapprehension that my criticism of the United Nations Secretariat for some reason has precluded addressing myself also to governmental iniquities, I may simply mention here that I am, as far as I know,

the only person to have drawn to public attention the facts and documents of the illicit secret agreement contracted between the United States Department of State and the United Nations Secretariat in 1948—a conspiracy which, with its infinite and tragic consequences, is described at some length in my book *Defeat of an Ideal*." (Letter, Hazzard to Jessup, March 14, 1974). A copy of this letter is held in Shirley Hazzard Papers, Rare Book and Manuscript Library, Columbia University.

14. Tony Judt, *When the Facts Change: Essays, 1995–2010* (New York: Penguin, 2015), 252.

15. It should also be noted that, as Lynn Hunt argues in her historical study of the development of international human rights, while "these NGOs frequently brought more pressure to bear on offending governments and did more to ameliorate famine, disease, and brutal treatment of dissidents and minorities than the United Nations itself, . . . almost all of them based their programs on the rights articulated in one or another part of the Universal Declaration." Lynn Hunt, *Inventing Human Rights: A History* (New York: Norton, 2007), 208.

16. See Mark Mazower on George Kennan's "denunciation of the escapism and wishful thinking that lay behind popular support for the United Nations" and his articulation of "a new 'realism' in thinking about international affairs." Mazower, *Governing*, 236.

17. Mazower outlines the development of the "Committee to Frame a World Constitution" in 1947 to address "the terrors of nuclear war" (232) as one response from those who "believed the United Nations had not gone far enough," (233) and notes also that the concern of participants at the 1955 Bandung Conference was "to speak out for a world whose basic survival was threatened not so much by the Cold War as by nuclear armageddon" (259).

18. "Pilgrimage," in Shirley Hazzard and Francis Steegmuller, *The Ancient Shore: Dispatches From Naples* (Chicago: University of Chicago Press, 2008), 23.

WE NEED SILENCE TO FIND OUT WHAT WE THINK

First published November 14, 1982, in the *New York Times Book Review*, 11, 28–29.

1. "Many brave men lived before Agamemnon, / But all went down unmourned, unhonoured into the smothering darkness / For lack of a minstrel to be their glory-giver." In *The Odes of Horace*, trans. James Michie (London: Rupert Hart-Davis, 1964), bk. 4, 247, 249.

2. Eugenio Montale, *It Depends: A Poet's Notebook*, trans. G. Singh (New York: New Directions, 1977), 29.

3. W. B. Yeats, "Samhain: 1905," in *Explorations*, ed. George Yeats (London: Macmillan, 1962), 199.

4. Quoted in *The Letters of Gustave Flaubert, 1857–1880*, ed. and trans. Francis Steegmuller (Cambridge, MA: Harvard University Press, 1982), xii.

5. "Veronese Before the Holy Tribunal (The Minutes of the Tribunal of the Inquisition Tribunal of Saturday 18 July 1573)," in *Literary Sources of Art History*, ed. and trans. E. G. Holt (Princeton, NJ: Princeton University Press, 1947), 129–132.

6. W. H. Auden, "The Novelist," in *Collected Poems*, ed. Edward Mendelson (London: Faber and Faber, 1976), 147.

7. Paul Valéry, "Entre deux mots il faut choisir le moindre," *Tel Quel* (Tome 1), cited in François Richaudeau, "Paul Valéry: Précurseur des Sciences du Langage," *Communication et Langages*, no. 18 (1973): 16.

8. T. S. Eliot, "East Coker" from "Four Quartets," in *The Complete Poems and Plays of T. S. Eliot* (London: Faber and Faber, 1982), 177.

9. Flaubert to George Sand, March 10, 1876, in Steegmuller, *Letters, 1857–1880*, 231.

10. Shirley Hazzard, "A Jaded Muse," in *From Parnassus: Essays in Honor of Jacques Barzun*, ed. Dora B. Weiner and William R. Keylor (New York: Harper and Row, 1976), 121–134. Hazzard notes that this was said "in conversation."

11. James Boswell, *Life of Johnson* (London: Oxford University Press, 1961), 689.

12. "To write in plain, vigorous language, one has to think fearlessly, and if one thinks fearlessly one cannot be politically orthodox." George Orwell, "The Prevention of Literature," in *The Orwell Reader: Fiction, Essays, Reportage* (New York: Harcourt, Brace and Company, 1956), 374.

13. Lucius Annaeus Seneca, "And I hold that no man has treated mankind worse than he who has studied philosophy as if it were some marketable trade, who lives in a different manner from that which he advises. For those who are liable to every fault which they castigate advertise themselves as patterns of useless training." Letter 108, "On the Approaches to Philosophy," in *Moral Epistles*, trans. Richard Gummere (Cambridge, MA: Harvard University Press, 1917–25), available at http://www.stoics.com/seneca_epistles_book_3.html.

14. Lord George Gordon Byron, "Don Juan," in *Byron: Poetical Works*, ed. Frederick Page and revised by John Jump (Oxford: Oxford University Press, 1989), Canto 3:697.

15. Jose Ortega y Gasset, "The Self and the Other," in *Dehumanization of Art and Other Essays on Art, Culture, and Literature*, trans. Willard R. Task (Princeton, NJ: Princeton University Press, 1968), 202.

16. Editor's note: I have been unable to trace the source of these quotations in Hazzard's papers or in the published works of Montale. It is likely that they were originally published in Italian and have not been republished.

17. "It is not pathetic messages that make us shed our best tears, but the miracle of a word in the right place." Jean Cocteau, *A Call to Order*, trans. Roll H. Myers (London: Faber and Gwyer, 1936), 153.

THE LONELY WORD

The Gauss Seminars: The Lonely Word were originally presented on April 27, April 29, and May 6, 1982, at Princeton University.

1. "Di un gatto sperduto," in Eugenio Montale, *It Depends: A Poet's Notebook*, trans. G. Singh (New York: New Directions, 1977), 86–87.

2. W. H. Auden, "The Poet and the City," in *The Dyer's Hand and Other Essays* (London: Faber and Faber, 1962), 78–80.

3. Editor's note: I have been unable to trace the source of this quotation in Hazzard's papers or in the published works of Montale. It is likely that it was originally published in an Italian journal or newspaper and has not been republished.

4. W. H. Auden, "The Shield of Achilles," in *W. H. Auden: Collected Poems*, ed. Edward Mendelson (London: Faber and Faber, 1976), 454–455.

5. W. H. Auden, "Secondary Epic," and "No, Plato, No," in *Auden: Collected Poems*, 455, 669.

6. John Wilmot, Earl of Rochester, "A Satire Against Reason and Mankind," in *The Complete Poems of John Wilmot, Earl of Rochester*, ed. David M. Veith (New Haven, CT: Yale University Press, 1974), 99.

7. Henry Reed, "The Naming of Parts," in *Henry Reed: Collected Poems*, ed. Jon Stallworthy (Manchester: Carcanet Press, 2007), 49.

8. Alfred, Lord Tennyson, "To Virgil," in *Poems and Plays* (London: Oxford University Press, 1973), 530.

9. Ibid., 531.

10. "And no—for enough, and more, wilt thou find eager to sing thy praises, Varus, and build the story of the grim war—now will I woo the rustic Muse on slender reed." Virgil, Eclogue VI, in *Virgil: Eclogues, Georgics, Aeneid*, trans. H. R. Fairclough (Cambridge, MA: Harvard University Press, 1978), 43.

11. Eugenio Montale, "La storia," I and II, in *Satura 1962–1970* (Milan: Arnoldo Mondadori, 1971), 51–53.

12. Werner Jaeger, *Paideia: The Ideals of Greek Culture*, vol. 1, *Archaic Greece: The Mind of Athens*, trans. Gilbert Highet (Oxford: Basil Blackwell, 1960), 35.

13. Paulinus to Ausonius, quoted in S. Dill, *Roman Society in the Last Century of the Western Empire* (London: 1898), 332.

14. W. B. Yeats, "Vacillation," in *W. B. Yeats: The Poems*, ed. Richard J. Finneran (London: Macmillan, 1983), 252.

15. St. Augustine, *Confessions*, trans. F. J. Sheed (Indianapolis: Hackett Publishing, 2006), bk. 1, chap. 13, 14–15.

16. Wordsworth, "Ode to Duty," in *Wordsworth Poems*, ed. W. E. Williams (Harmondsworth: Penguin, 1985), 65.

17. Jean Seznec, *The Survival of the Pagan Gods: The Mythological Tradition and its Place in Renaissance Humanism and Art*, trans. Barbara F. Sessions (Princeton,

NJ: Princeton University Press, 1953); "Virtue reconciled with Pleasure," chap. 5, in Edgar Wind, *Pagan Mysteries in the Renaissance* (London: Faber and Faber 1958), 78–88.

18. Alexander Pope, "The Dunciad," in *The Poetical Works of Alexander Pope*, ed. Herbert Davis (Oxford: Oxford University Press, 1983), 467.

19. William Shakespeare, *Hamlet*, act 5, scene 2, lines 212–213.

20. William Shakespeare, Sonnet 15, in *Shakespeare's Sonnets*, ed. Katherine Duncan-Jones (London: A and C Black, 2010), 141.

21. Walter Scott, entry March 14, 1836, in *Journal of Walter Scott, 1825–1826*, ed. J. G. Tair (London: 1939), 135. Quoted in *Jane Austen: The Critical Heritage*, ed. B. C. Southam, 2 vols. (London: Routledge, 1968), 1:106.

22. Robert Burns, "O Why Should Honest Poverty," in *Burns in English: Select Poems of Robert Burns*, ed. Alexander Corbett (Glasgow, 1892), 109–110.

23. Lord George Gordon Byron, "Don Juan," in *Byron: Poetical Works*, ed. Frederick Page and revised by John Jump (Oxford: Oxford University Press, 1989), Canto 11, 799.

24. Thomas Medwin, *Journal of the Conversations of Lord Byron: Noted During a Residence with His Lordship at Pisa in the Years 1821 and 1822* (New York, 1824), 112.

25. Byron, "Don Juan," in *Byron: Poetical Works*, Canto 6, 731.

26. William Shakespeare, *Richard II*, act 3, scene 2.

27. Translation is Hazzard's. Cf "And [the Romantics] do not see that this great ideal of our times—this intimate understanding of our heart, analyzing, predicting, identifying each of its tiny emotions one by one, in short this psychological art—destroys the illusion without which poetry will never exist." In Giacomo Leopardi, *Zibaldone: The Notebooks of Leopardi*, trans. and ed. Michael Caesar and Franco D'Intino (London: Penguin, 2013), 16.

28. Eugenio Montale, *Otherwise: Last and First Poems of Eugenio Montale* (New York: Random House, 1984), 70.

29. Eugenio Montale, "La fama e il fisco," in *Diario del '71 e del '72* (Milan: Arnoldo Mondadori, 1973), 75.

30. Arthur Hugh Clough, "Easter Day. Naples 1849," in *Poems of Arthur Hugh Clough*, ed. F. L. Mulhauser (London: Clarendon Press, 1974), 201.

31. Charles Baudelaire, "Spleen," in *Fleurs du Mal*, ed. Enid Starkie (Oxford: Basil Blackwell, 1942), 73.

32. Victor Brombert, *The Romantic Prison* (Princeton, NJ: Princeton University Press, 1978), 5.

33. T. S. Eliot, "Gerontion," in *The Complete Poems and Plays of T. S. Eliot* (London: Faber and Faber, 1982), 38.

34. Edwin Muir, "The Combat," in Edwin Muir, *Collected Poems* (London: Faber and Faber, 1960), 179–180.

35. W. B. Yeats, "The Statues," in Finneran, *Yeats*, 337.

36. W. B. Yeats, "The Municipal Gallery Revisited," in Finneran, *Yeats*, 320.

37. W. H. Auden, "Letter to Lord Byron," in *Auden: Collected Poems*, 93.

38. Editor's note: I have been unable to trace the source of this quotation in Hazzard's papers or in the published works of Montale. It is likely that it was originally published in an Italian journal or newspaper and has not been republished.

39. Cecil Day Lewis, "The Dead," in *The Complete Poems* (Stanford, CA: Stanford University Press, 1992), 338–339.

40. Eugenio Montale, Nobel Prize acceptance speech, 1975, available at http://www.nobelprize.org/nobel_prizes/literature/laureates/1975/montale-lecture-i.html.

41. Eugenio Montale, "Per finire," in *Diario del '71 e del '72* (Milan: Mondadori, 1973).

42. Ibid.

43. Tennyson, "To Virgil," in *Tennyson: Poems and Plays*, 530.

44. Montale, *It Depends*, 28–29.

45. Jaeger, *Paideia*, 13.

46. W. B. Yeats, "Mehru," from "Supernatural Songs," in Finneran, *Yeats*, 289.

47. Aleksandr Solzhenitsyn, Nobel Prize Acceptance Speech, available at http://www.nobelprize.org/nobel_prizes/literature/laureates/1970/solzhenitsyn-lecture.html.

48. Montale, Nobel Prize Acceptance Speech.

49. Walt Whitman, preface to *Leaves of Grass*, ed. David S. Reynolds (Oxford: Oxford University Press, 2005), v.

50. Tennyson, "To Virgil," in *Tennyson: Poems and Plays*, 530.

51. Martin Heidegger, *What is Philosophy?*, trans. William Kluback and Jean T. Wilde (London: Vision Press, 1956), 45.

52. Samuel Taylor Coleridge, "Shakespeare, A Poet Generally," in *The Literary Remains of Samuel Taylor Coleridge*, ed. Henry Nelson Coleridge (London: 1836), 59.

53. W. H. Auden, "In Memory of W. B. Yeats," in *Auden: Collected Poems*, 197.

54. W. B. Yeats, "Samhain: 1905," in *Explorations*, ed. Georgie Yeats (London: Macmillan, 1962).

55. Quoted in *The Letters of Gustave Flaubert, 1857–1880*, ed. and trans. Francis Steegmuller (Cambridge, MA: Harvard University Press, 1982), xii.

56. Norman Douglas, *Three of Them* (London: Chatto and Windus, 1930), 40–41.

57. Pater was a nineteenth-century author and art critic. Douglas, *Three of Them*, 40–41.

58. Paul Valéry, "Entre deux mots il faut choisir le moindre," *Tel Quel* (Tome 1), cited in François Richaudeau, "Paul Valéry: Précurseur des Sciences du Langage," *Communication et Langages* 18, no.18 (1973): 16.

59. Broadcast, June 18, 1940, available at http://www.bbc.co.uk/archive/battleofbritain/11428.shtml.

60. Broadcast, December 11, 1936, available at http://www.bbc.co.uk/archive/edward_viii/12937.shtml.

61. T. S. Eliot, "East Coker," in *The Complete Poems and Plays of T. S. Eliot* (London: Faber and Faber, 1982), 177.

62. Flaubert to George Sand, March 10, 1876, in Steegmuller, *Letters, 1857–1880*, 231.

63. William Shakespeare, Sonnet 25, in *Shakespeare's Sonnets*, ed. Katherine Duncan-Jones (London: A and C Black, 2010), 161; *Richard III*, act 1, scene 4, line 55; *Antony and Cleopatra*, act 4, scene 10, line 25.

64. Shirley Hazzard, "A Jaded Muse," in *From Parnassus: Essays in Honor of Jacques Barzun*, ed. Dora B. Weiner and William R. Keylor (New York: Harper and Row, 1976), 121–134. Hazzard uses this quotation from Barzun as epitaph, noting that it was said "in conversation."

65. Samuel Johnson, "The Preface to the Dictionary," in *Samuel Johnson: Selected Writings* (Cambridge, MA: Harvard University Press, 2009), ProQuest ebrary, December 4, 2014, 246.

66. James Boswell, *Life of Johnson* (London: Oxford University Press, 1961), 689.

67. Marguerite, Countess of Blessington, *A Journal of Conversations with Lord Byron* (Boston: 1858), 46.

68. Alexander Pope, "Dialogue II," from "Epilogue to the Satires in Two Dialogues," in *Pope: Poetical Works*, ed. Herbert Davis (Oxford: Oxford University Press, 1983), 421.

69. George Eliot, *Middlemarch* (London: Penguin, 2003), 302.

70. Ibid., 298.

71. Ibid., 199.

72. Ibid., 71.

73. Ibid., 310.

74. Ibid., 312.

75. Ibid., 141.

76. Catullus, Fragment LXXXIV, in *The Poems and Fragments of Catullus*, trans. Robinson Ellis (London: 1871), 91 (Project Gutenberg).

77. "So wise he judges it to fly from pain / However, and to scape his punishment. So judge thou still, presumptuous, till the wrauth, / Which thou incurr'st by flying, meet thy flight / Sevenfold, and scourge that wisdom back to

Hell," in John Milton, *Paradise Lost*, ed. Dennis Danielson (Toronto: Broadview Press, 2012), bk. 4, lines 910–914. Hazzard's paraphrase.

78. William Empson, *Seven Types of Ambiguity* (New York: New Directions, 1966), 127.

79. Anthony Trollope, *Phineas Redux*, (Oxford: Oxford University Press, 2011), 527.

80. Eliot, *Middlemarch*, 99.

81. Seneca, "And I hold that no man has treated mankind worse than he who has studied philosophy as if it were some marketable trade, who lives in a different manner from that which he advises. For those who are liable to every fault which they castigate advertise themselves as patterns of useless training," from Letter 108, "On the Approaches to Philosophy," in *Moral Epistles*, trans. Richard Gummere (Cambridge, MA: Harvard University Press, 1917–25): available at http://www.stoics.com/seneca_epistles_book_3.html.

82. William Shakespeare, *Richard II*, act 5, scene 4.

83. G. K. Chesterton, "Lepanto," in *Collected Works* (San Francisco: Ignatius Press, 1994), 10:550.

84. Ford Madox Ford, *Parade's End* (New York: Knopf, 1961), 234.

85. Byron, "Don Juan" in *Byron: Poetical Works*, Dedication 9, 636.

86. Alexander Pope, "Elegy to the Memory of an Unfortunate Lady," in *The Poems of Alexander Pope: A One Volume Edition of The Twickenham Pope*, ed. John Butt (London: Routledge, 1989), 262.

87. Byron, "Don Juan," *Byron: Poetical Works*, Canto 14, 822.

88. Lord George Gordon Byron, "Childe Harold's Pilgrimage" in *Byron: Poetical Works*, 245.

89. "During my life, I have passionately loved, / Cimarosa / Mozart / and Shakespeare only." Stendhal, *Memoirs of an Egoist*, ed. David Ellis (London: Chatto and Windus, 1975), 88.

90. John Keats, Letter to Fanny Brawne, February (?) 1820, in *Letters of John Keats*, vol. 2, *1819–1821*, ed. Hyder Edward Rollins (Cambridge: Cambridge University Press, 1958), 263.

91. Translation is Hazzard's. See n. 19 in Giacomo Leopardi, *Canti*, trans. Jonathan Galassi (New York: Farrar, Straus and Giroux, 2011), 382.

92. Translation is Hazzard's. Giacomo Leopardi, "La Ginestra," in Leopardi, *Canti*, 290.

93. Translation is Hazzard's. Leopardi, *Canti*, 290.

94. "Many brave men lived before Agamemnon, / But all went down unmourned, unhonoured into the smothering darkness / For lack of a minstrel to be their glory-giver." *Odes of Horace*, 247, 249; Montale, *It Depends*, 29–32.

95. William Shakespeare, "Sonnet 65," in *Shakespeare's Sonnets*, ed. Katherine Duncan-Jones (London: A & C Black, 2010), 241.

96. Byron, "Don Juan" in *Byron: Poetical Works*, Canto 3, 696.

97. The more usual translation is by Richard Lourie, "You who wronged a simple man/ . . . Do not feel safe. The poet remembers," from "You Who Wronged," in Czesław Miłosz, *The Collected Poems, 1931–1947* (New York: Ecco Press, 1988), 106.

98. James Kirkup, "On a Tanaka by Ochi-Ai Naobumi (1861–1903)," *New Yorker*, October 3 1959, 46.

99. "But sweet desire hurries me over the lonely steeps of Parnassus." Virgil, *Georgics*, in *Virgil: Eclogues, Georgics, Aeneid* 1–6, trans. H. R. Fairclough (Cambridge, MA: Harvard University Press, 1978), bk. 3, 174–175.

100. Francesco Petrarch, *Some Love Songs of Petrarch*, trans. William Dudley Foulke (Oxford; Oxford University Press, 1915), 225, available at http://oll.libertyfund.org/titles/1341.

101. Quoted in R. Z. Sheppard, "Truth and Consequences," *Time*, January 18, 1982, 77.

102. Guido Gozzano, *The Man I Pretend to Be: "The Colloquies" and Selected Poems of Guido Gozzano* (Princeton, NJ: Princeton University Press, 2014), 66–97.

103. Eugenio Montale, "The Lemons," in *Montale: Collected Poems, 1920–1954*, trans. Jonathan Galassi (New York: Farrar, Straus and Giroux, 2012), 8–11.

104. Eugenio Montale, "La mia musa," in *Diario*, 30.

105. "The posthumous castigation of Shelley began the . . . day [after the public announcement of his death] when the conservative *Courier* announced, 'Shelley, the writer of some infidel poetry, has been drowned; now he knows whether there is a God or no,'" in James Bieri, *Percy Shelley: A Biography—Exile of Unfulfilled Renown, 1816–1822* (Newark: University of Delaware Press, 2005), 338.

106. Wallace Stevens, "Mozart, 1935," in *The Collected Poems of Wallace Stevens* (New York: Knopf, 2011), 132.

107. W. H. Auden, "In Memory of W. B. Yeats," in *W. H. Auden: Selected Poems*, ed. Edward Mendelson, exp. ed. (New York: Vintage International, 2007), 90.

108. W. H. Auden, "The Poet and The City," in *The Dyer's Hand*, 85.

109. Randall Jarrell, "The Obscurity of the Poet," in *Poetry and the Age* (New York: Knopf, 1953), 34. "But this has been said, better than it is ever again likely to be said, by the greatest of writers of this century, Marcel Proust; and I should like to finish this lecture by quoting his sentences: 'All that we can say is that everything is arranged in this life as though we entered it carrying the burden of obligations contracted in a former life; there is no reason inherent in the conditions of life on this earth that can make us consider ourselves obliged to do good, to be fastidious, to be polite even, nor make the talented artist consider himself obliged to begin over again a score of times a piece of work the admiration aroused by which will matter little to his body devoured by worms,

like the patch of yellow wall painted with so much knowledge and skill by an artist who must remain forever unknown and is barely identified under the name of Vermeer. All these obligations which have not their sanction in our present life seem to belong to a different world, founded upon kindness, scrupulosity, self-sacrifice, a world entirely different from this, which we leave in order to be born into this world, before perhaps returning to the other to live once again beneath the sway of those unknown laws which we have obeyed because we bore their precepts in our hearts, knowing not whose hand had traced them there—those laws to which every profound work of the intellect brings us nearer and which are invisible only—and still!—to fools' " (35).

110. "A reconciliation with [a] death." John Marston, *Antonio's Revenge*, ed. Reavley Gair (Manchester: Manchester University Press, 1978), 62.

111. Nicanor Parra, *Poems and Antipoems*, ed. Miller Williams, trans. Fernando Alegría and others (New York: New Directions, 1967), 148.

112. Dubuffet's comment is quoted in John Russell, "Art View: The Many Aspects of Jean Dubuffet," *New York Times*, May 26, 1985. available at http://www.nytimes.com/1985/05/26/arts/art-view-the-many-aspects-of-jean-dubuffet.html.

113. Jean Dubuffet, *Jean Dubuffet: A Retrospective* (New York: Solomon R. Guggenheim Foundation, 1973).

114. Marcel Proust, *The Captive*, in *Remembrance of Things Past*, trans. C.K. Scott Moncrieff and Terence Kilmartin, with the assistance of Andreas Mayor (Harmondsworth: Penguin, 1981), 386.

115. Samuel Johnson, *The Rambler*, no. 146, Saturday, August 10, 1751 (Troy, NY: Parfraets, 1903), 211.

116. Byron, "Don Juan," in *Byron: Poetical Works*, Canto 11, 795.

117. Leopardi, *Zibaldone*, 180.

118. Eugenio Montale, "The Artist's Solitude," in *The Second Life of Art: Selected Essays of Eugenio Montale*, ed. and trans. Jonathan Galassi (New York: Ecco, 1982), 25–28.

A MIND LIKE A BLADE: REVIEW OF MURIEL SPARK, *COLLECTED STORIES I* AND *THE PUBLIC IMAGE*

First published September, 29, 1968, in the *New York Times Book Review*, 1.

1. "Sybil was precocious, her brain was like a blade." From "Bang-bang You're Dead," in Muriel Spark, *Collected Stories I* (London: Macmillan, 1967), 80.

2. Palinurus (Cyril Connolly), *The Unquiet Grave* (London: Penguin, 1999), 21.

3. "Come Along, Marjorie," in Spark, *Collected Stories*, 206.

4. "Bang-bang You're Dead," in Spark, *Collected Stories*, 97.

5. Spark, *Collected Stories*, 110.

6. Muriel Spark, *The Public Image* (London: Virago, 1979), 67.
7. "The Father's Daughters," in Spark, *Collected Stories*, 286.

REVIEW OF JEAN RHYS, *QUARTET*

First published April 11, 1971, in the *New York Times Book Review*, 6.

1. Jean Rhys, *Quartet* (New York: Norton, 1997), 130.
2. Ibid., 60.
3. Ibid., 61.
4. Ibid., 61.
5. Ibid., 81.
6. Ibid., 118.
7. Ibid., 114.
8. Ibid., 113.
9. Ibid., 64.
10. Ibid., 110.
11. "Il est assez puni par son sort rigoreaux; / Et c'est être innocent que d'être malheureux." Jean de La Fontaine, "Élégies I—Pour M. Fouquet: Aux Nymphes de Vaux," in *Oeuvres Complètes de Jean de La Fontaine*, ed. Jean de La Fontaine and Charles Athanase Walckenaer (Paris: 1835), 518.

THE LASTING SICKNESS OF NAPLES: REVIEW OF MATILDE SERAO, *IL VENTRE DI NAPOLI*

First published December 21, 1973, in the *Times Literary Supplement*, 1558.

1. Translation is Hazzard's. Giacomo Leopardi, "La Ginestra," in *Canti*, trans. Shirley Hazzard, ed. Jonathan Galassi (New York: Farrar, Straus and Giroux, 2011), 286.
2. See the references to "La Topaia" in Giacomo Leopardi, *Paralipomeni della Batracomiomachia* (Paris, 1842), 35.
3. Curzio Malaparte, *The Skin*, trans. David Moore (New York: New York Review Books, 2013), 39.
4. Matilde Serao, *Il Ventre di Napoli* (Scrivere ebook, 2012), part 1, chap. 1, "Bisogna sventare Napoli," 6.
5. Serao, *Il Ventre*, part 1, chap. 1, "Bisogna sventare Napoli," 12; part 1, chap. 2, "Quello che guadagnano," 72.
6. Arthur Hugh Clough, "Easter Day. Naples 1849," in *Poems of Arthur Hugh Clough*, ed. F. L. Mulhauser (London: Clarendon Press, 1974), 199.
7. Serao, *Il Ventre*, part 1, chap. 1, "Bisogna sventare Napoli," 4.
8. Serao, *Il Ventre*, part 2, "Adesso," chap. 1, "Il paravento," 49–50.
9. Serao, *Il Ventre*, part 1, chap. 1, "Bisogna sventare Napoli," 7.

THE NEW NOVEL BY THE NEW NOBEL PRIZE WINNER: REVIEW OF PATRICK WHITE, *THE EYE OF THE STORM*

First published January 6, 1974, in the *New York Times Book Review*, 1, 12.

1. Patrick White, *The Eye of the Storm* (New York: Picador, 2012), 85, 72, 121.
2. Ibid., 72, 367, 79.
3. Ibid., 414.
4. Ibid., 500.
5. Ibid., 135.
6. Ibid., 285.
7. Ibid., 64, 44–45.
8. Ibid., 561.
9. Ibid., 93.
10. Ibid., 415.
11. Ibid., 424.
12. Ibid., 424.
13. Ibid., 414.
14. Ibid., 451.
15. Ibid., 300.
16. Ibid., 465, 466.
17. W. H. Auden, "The Novelist," in *W. H. Auden: Collected Poems*, ed. Edward Mendelson (London: Faber and Faber, 1976), 147.
18. White, *Eye*, 93.
19. Patrick White, *Voss* (New York: Viking, 1957), 234.
20. The Nobel citation for White is available at http://www.nobelprize.org/nobel_prizes/literature/laureates/1973/presentation-speech.html.

ORDINARY PEOPLE: REVIEW OF BARBARA PYM, *QUARTET IN AUTUMN* AND *EXCELLENT WOMEN*

First published September 10, 1978, in *Book Review*, 2.

1. George Eliot, *Scenes of Clerical Life* (Harmondsworth, UK: Penguin, 1973), 81.
2. Barbara Pym, *Excellent Women* (Harmondsworth, UK: Penguin, 1986), 105.
3. Ibid., 69.

TRANSLATING PROUST

First published in *The Proust Project*, ed. André Aciman (New York: Farrar, Straus and Giroux, 1994), 174–181.

1. Quoted in "Reflections: Gustave Flaubert's Correspondence," in *The Letters of Gustave Flaubert, 1830–1857*, ed. Francis Steegmuller (London: Faber and Faber, 1980), xii.

2. George D. Painter, *Marcel Proust: A Biography*, vol. 2 (London: Chatto and Windus, 1959), 351.

3. François Guizot, "Guizot's Preface," in Edward Gibbon, *Guizot's Gibbon: History of the Decline and Fall of the Roman Empire* (Oxford, 1841), xiv–xv.

4. Marcel Proust, *Remembrance of Things Past*, trans. C. K. Scott-Moncrieff (New York: Random House, 1932), vol. 2, 711.

5. Marcel Proust, *Remembrance of Things Past*, trans. C. K. Scott Moncrieff, Terence Kilmartin, and Andreas Mayor (Harmondsworth, UK: Penguin, 1983), vol. 3, 477.

6. Marcel Proust, *In Search of Lost Time*, trans. C. K. Scott Moncrieff and Terence Kilmartin, rev. D. J. Enright (London: Chatto and Windus, 1992), vol. 3, 685.

7. Marcel Proust, *In Search of Lost Time: The Prisoner and The Fugitive*, trans. Christopher Prendergast, Carol Clark, and Peter Collier (London: Penguin, 2003), 474.

8. Gustave Flaubert, "Letter to Louise Colet," December 16, 1852, in Steegmuller, *Letters*, 176.

INTRODUCTION TO GEOFFREY SCOTT'S *THE PORTRAIT OF ZÉLIDE*

First published in Geoffrey Scott, *The Portrait of Zélide* (New York: Turtle Point Press, 1997), ix–xviii.

1. Geoffrey Scott, *The Portrait of Zélide* (New York: Helen Marx, 1997), 36.

2. Ibid., 197.

3. Ibid., 40.

4. "My Last Duchess," in *Robert Browning: Selected Poems*, ed. John Woolford, Daniel Karlan, and Joseph Phelan (Abingdon, UK: Pearson, 2010), 199–200.

5. Scott, *Zélide*, 29.

6. Ibid., 12.

7. Geoffrey Scott, introduction to *Four Tales by Zélide*, by Madame de Charrière, trans. and ed. Geoffrey Scott (London: Constable, 1925), xvii–xviii.

8. Scott, *Zélide*, 34.

9. Ibid., 101.

10. Ibid., 130–131.

11. Ibid., 190–191.

12. Ibid., 211.

INTRODUCTION TO IRIS ORIGO'S *LEOPARDI: A STUDY IN SOLITUDE*

First published in Iris Origo, *Leopardi: A Study in Solitude* (New York: Helen Marx, 2000), 3–12.

1. Iris Origo, *Leopari: A Study in Solitude* (New York: Helen Marx, 1999), 32.
2. Ibid., 60.
3. Niccolò Machiavelli, "Letter to Francesco Vettori, 15 December 1513," quoted in the introduction to *The Prince*, trans. W. K. Marriott (Rockville, MD: Arc Manor, 2007), 5–13, 9.
4. Giacomo Leopardi, *Epistolario*, to Giordano, March 21, 1817, quoted in Origo, *Leopardi*, 62. Origo's translation is modified slightly by Hazzard.
5. Translation is Hazzard's. "A Silvia," in Leopardi, *Canti*, 174.
6. Translation is Hazzard's. "Le Ricordanze," in Leopardi, *Canti*, 182.
7. Translation is Hazzard's (but based loosely on that by John Heath-Stubbs). "La Sera del Dì di Festa," in Leopardi, *Canti*, 108. Cf. trans. John Heath-Stubbs, *Poems From Giacomo Leopardi* (London: John Lehmann, 1946), 20.
8. W. H. Auden, "In Memory of W. B. Yeats," in *Collected Poems*, ed. Edward Mendelson (London: Faber and Faber, 1976), 197.
9. Translation is Hazzard's. Leopardi, "On the Monument to Dante Being Erected in Florence," in *Canti*, 24.
10. Quoted in Walter Pater, "Winckelmann," in *The Renaissance* (New York: Modern Library 1873), 148.
11. The epigraph to Goethe's *Italian Journey*, trans. Robert R. Heitner, in *Goethe: The Collected Works* (Princeton: Princeton University Press, 1989), vol. 6., n.p.
12. W. H. Auden, introduction to *The Complete Poems of C. P. Cavafy*, trans. Rae Dalven (New York: Harcourt, Brace, 1961), viii–xi.
13. Rodrigo Caro, *La canción a las ruinas de Itálica* (Bogotá: Editorial Voluntad, 1947).
14. "Il tramonto della luna," in Leopardi, *Canti*, 282.

WILLIAM MAXWELL

First published in *A William Maxwell Portrait: Memories and Appreciations*, ed. Charles Baxter, Michael Collier, and Edward Hirsch (New York: Norton, 2004), 117–122.

1. Jean Cocteau, *The Difficulty of Being* (New York: Melville House, 2013).
2. William Shakespeare, *Cymbeline*, act 4, scene 2.
3. Graham Greene, *A Sort of Life* (London: Vintage, 1999), 134.

4. W. B. Yeats, "Vacillation," in *The Collected Poems of W. B. Yeats*, ed. and annotated by Richard J. Finneran (London: Macmillan, 1950), 284.

5. William Maxwell, *The Chateau* (London: Harvill Press, 2000), 345.

THE PATRON SAINT OF THE UN IS PONTIUS PILATE

First published February 23, 1974, in the *New York Times*, 31.

1. "UN Unit Drops Support of Conference on Torture," *New York Times*, December 4, 1973, 2.

2. "Kriesky Firm on Closing It: UN Says It Has No Authority to Run Jews' Transit Camp," *International Herald Tribune*, October 4, 1973, 1.

3. Editor's note: These quotations are not from published news sources. They are likely to be from internal UN documents, but copies were not found in Hazzard's papers.

4. Editor's note: This quotation is likely to be from an internal UN document, but no copy was found in Hazzard's papers.

5. Aleksandr Solzhenitsyn, Nobel Lecture, available at http://www.nobelprize.org/nobel_prizes/literature/laureates/1970/solzhenitsyn-lecture.html.

"GULAG" AND THE MEN OF PEACE

First published in August 25, 1974, in the *New York Times*, 446.

1. United Nations, Chapter XV: The Secretariat, Article 100, http://www.un.org/en/documents/charter/chapter15.shtml.

2. United Nations, Universal Declaration of Human Rights, Article 19, http://www.un.org/en/documents/udhr/index.shtml#a19.

3. United Nations Press Release SG/SM/2033, July 5, 1974, 2–3. Copy of Press Release held in Shirley Hazzard Papers, Rare Book and Manuscript Library, Columbia University in the City of New York.

4. UN Press Release SG/SM/2033, 2.

5. "UN Chief Gives Mild Retort to Solzhenitsyn," *International Herald Tribune*, August 28, 1972.

6. George Orwell, *Nineteen Eighty-Four* (London: Penguin, 1989), 223.

7. Aleksandr Solzhenitsyn, Nobel Lecture, available at http://www.nobelprize.org/nobel_prizes/literature/laureates/1970/solzhenitsyn-lecture.html.

8. Aleksandr Solzhenitsyn, "The Prison Industry," part 1 in *The Gulag Archipelago* (London: Collins, 1974), 17.

9. Copy of letter from Jerzy Kosinski, PEN president, to Kurt Waldheim, August 1, 1974, held in Shirley Hazzard Papers, Rare Book and Manuscript Library, Columbia University.

10. "Confucius Loses Face at UN," *Times* (London), September 19, 1974, 20.

THE UNITED NATIONS: WHERE GOVERNMENTS GO TO CHURCH

First published March 1, 1975, in the *New Republic*, 11–14.

1. James McDonald, "Letter of Resignation of James G. McDonald, HCR (Jewish and other) coming from Germany addressed to the Secretary-General of the League of Nations," London, December 27, 1935, in Victor Yves Ghebali and Catherine Ghebali, *A Repertoire of League of Nations Serial Documents, 1919–1947* (Dobbs Ferry, NY: Oceana Publications, 1973), x. McDonald's resignation letter is available at http://www.jta.org/1935/12/30/archive/mcdonald-resigns-urges-league-intervention-for-reich-jews.

2. Nan Robertson, "UNESCO is Facing Bitter Backlash," *New York Times*, December 8, 1974, 5.

3. John Maynard Keynes, *Essays in Persuasion* (London: Rupert Hart-Davis, 1952), 21.

4. Kathleen Telsch, in "UN Assembly Session Produces 150 Resolutions and a Treaty to Protect Diplomats," reports that "During the session, the 135 member nations . . . approved a $540,473,000 United Nations budget for 1974 and 1975." Hazzard has noted on the clipping: "'Regular' budget only," *New York Times*, December 23, 1973, 4. Shirley Hazzard Papers, Rare Book and Manuscript Library, Columbia University.

5. Aleksandr Solzhenitsyn, Nobel Lecture, available at http://www.nobelprize.org/nobel_prizes/literature/laureates/1970/solzhenitsyn-lecture.html.

6. Keynes, *Essays in Persuasion*, 356.

7. Richard J. Barnet and Ronald E. Müller, *Global Reach: The Power of Multinational Corporations* (New York: Simon and Schuster, 1974), 283.

8. Hubert Miles Gladwyn Jebb, Baron Gladwyn, *The Memoirs of Lord Gladwyn* (London: Weidenfeld and Nicholson, 1972), 257–258.

9. "New Rule Raises Limits on Cargo: Load-line Convention Goes into Effect Today," *New York Times*, July 21, 1968, 244.

10. This matter is the subject of Hazzard's first monograph on the UN, *Defeat of an Ideal: A Study of the Self-Destruction of the United Nations* (New York: Little, Brown, 1973).

11. Alice Ritchie, *The Peacemakers* (London: Hogarth Press, 1928), 77.

12. Ibid., 78.

13. Letter, André Lewin to F. R. Buckley, November 5, 1974, Shirley Hazzard Papers, Rare Book and Manuscript Library, Columbia University.

14. "UN Unit Drops Support of Conference on Torture," *New York Times*, December 4, 1973, 2.

15. Kathleen Telsch, "UN Rights Group is Under Attack," *New York Times*, March 10, 1974: 1, 25.

16. Seymour Maxwell Finger and John Mugno, *The Politics of Staffing the*

UN Secretariat (New York: The Ralph Bunche Institute on the United Nations, the Graduate School and University Center of the City University of New York, 1974).

17. Ibid., 44.

18. Ibid., 49.

19. Shirley Hazzard, *Defeat of an Ideal: A Study of the Self-Destruction of the United Nations* (New York: Little, Brown, 1973), 247.

20. "Dante says that there can be no real knowledge if what has been learned is not retained," quoted in Niccolò Machiavelli, *The Prince*, ed. Quentin Skinner and Russell Price (Cambridge: Cambridge University Press, 1988), 93.

THE LEAGUE OF FRIGHTENED MEN: WHY THE UN IS SO USELESS

First published January 19, 1980, in the *New Republic*, 17–20.

1. Christopher Wren, "Waldheim Cuts Mission Short after Khomeini Refuses a Meeting," *New York Times*, January 4, 1980: A1, A4.

2. "Kurt Waldheim interviewed by Barbara Walters and Lou Cioffi," *ABC News: Issues and Answers*, January 6, 1980, 13. Transcript held in Shirley Hazzard Papers, Rare Book and Manuscript Library, Columbia University.

3. *New York Times*, December 23, 1979, 29.

4. The Pahlavi Prize is mentioned in Albin Krebs, "Notes on People," *New York Times*, June 6, 1978, C9.

5. See http://www.thecanadianencyclopedia.ca/en/article/maurice-frederick-strong/.

6. Christopher S. Wren, "Waldheim, in Iran, Discourages Hopes for Breakthrough," *New York Times*, January 2, 1980, A1.

7. This event was also recorded in "Plight of Cambodians," *International Herald Tribune*, October 20–21, 1979. Clipping held in Shirley Hazzard Papers, Rare Book and Manuscript Library, Columbia University.

8. Kathleen Telsch, "Shevchenko Quits UN Post, Says He'll Stay in US," *New York Times* April 27, 1978, A11.

9. Iain Guest, "UN Aide Is Censured in Art Scandal," *International Herald Tribune*, October 27–28, 1979.

10. Aleksandr Solzhenitsyn, Nobel Lecture, available at http://www.nobelprize.org/nobel_prizes/literature/laureates/1970/solzhenitsyn-lecture.html.

11. *New York Times*, September 12, 1977, 8.

12. "Russians Mark Human Rights Day," *New York Times*, December 11, 1978.

13. Editor's note: The exact quotation was not found, but the following passage is marked in Shirley Hazzard's papers: "The Secretariat is a mess, declared a high ranking US official. He said there were no clear lines of authority or precise delineation of work in the Department of Economic and Social Affairs." Kathleen

Teltsch, "UN is Reorganizing to Aid Poor Nations," *New York Times*, February 3, 1978, A10. Shirley Hazzard Papers, Rare Book and Manuscript Library, Columbia University.

14. United States Senate Committee on Government Operations, *US Participation in International Organizations*, Doc. 95–50, 95th Cong., 1st sess., February 1977. Printed for the use of the Committee on Government Operations, (Washington: US Government Printing Office, 1977), 53–54. Copy held in Shirley Hazzard Papers, Rare Book and Manuscript Library, Columbia University.

15. Ronald Kessler, "UN System, Claiming Deficits, Has $1.4 Billion in Bank," *Washington Post*, June 17, 1979, A1, A8, A9.

16. Ronald Kessler, "After Report of $1.4-Billion Surplus: US House Panels to Probe UN Finances," *Washington Post*, June 20, 1979.

17. This matter is the subject of Hazzard's first monograph on the United Nations, *Defeat of an Ideal: A Study of the Self-Destruction of the United Nations* (New York: Little, Brown, 1973).

18. Kathleen Telsch, "UN Faces Rare Labor Turmoil and Fears the Unrest Runs Deep," *New York Times*, February 5, 1979, A4; "All Isn't Peace and Brotherhood Inside the United Nations," *Washington Post*, February 18, 1979, A4.

19. John Bunyan, *The Pilgrim's Progress* (London: Oxford University Press, 1932), 65.

UNHELPFUL: WALDHEIM'S LATEST DEBACLE

First published April 12, 1980, in the *New Republic*, 10–13.

1. U Thant, "Address Delivered by the Secretary-General of the United Nations, U Thant, in Commemoration of the Twentieth Anniversary of the Adoption of the Universal Declaration of Human Rights," in *Final Act of the International Conference on Human Rights, Teheran*, April 22–May 13, 1968, A /CONF.32/41 (New York: United Nations, 1968), 34–35.

2. "At Women's Parley, Gala Soothes Animosities—Some, Anyway," *New York Times*, June 22, 1975, 48.

3. "Panel Presses Iran on Seeing Hostages, But There Is Confusion on Timing," *New York Times*, February 29, 1980, A1.

4. "Panel Presses Iran," *New York Times*, A5.

5. Myra MacPherson, "Waldheim: The UN's Muted Peacekeeper Amid the Passions," *Washington Post*, January 18, 1980, B6.

6. John F. Kennedy, Inaugural Presidential Address, January 20, 1961: "To that world assembly of sovereign states, the United Nations, our last best hope in an age where the instruments of war have far outpaced the instruments of peace, we renew our pledge of support: to prevent it from becoming merely a forum for invective; to strengthen its shield of the new and the weak; and to enlarge the area in which

its writ may run." The full text of Kennedy's speech is available at http://www.presidency.ucsb.edu/ws/?pid-8032.

7. Kathleen Telsch, "UN Rights Group Is Under Attack," *New York Times*, March 10, 1974, 1, 25.

8. Bernard Nossiter, "Waldheim Says UN Panel Is only Suspending Its Work: 'Same Old Problem' with Militants," *New York Times*, March 11, 1980, A12.

9. "Transcript of the President's News Conference on Foreign and Domestic Matters," *New York Times*, February 14, 1980, A16.

10. Editor's note: The source for this quotation was not found. It is likely to be from an internal UN memo, but was not located among Hazzard's papers.

11. Bernard Nossiter, "Problems for UN Aid Plans," *New York Times*, March 29, 1980, 22.

12. Editor's note: The source for this quotation was not found. It is likely to be from an internal UN memo, but was not located among Hazzard's papers.

13. Christopher Wren, "Waldheim, in Iran, Plays Down Hope for Breakthrough," *New York Times*, January 2, 1980, 1, 10. See also MacPherson, "Waldheim," B6.

14. Bernard Nossiter, "Waldheim and Aides Are Reported Drafting Rules for Iran Inquiry," *New York Times*, February 15, 1980, A1, A10.

15. John Kifner, "Effort to Free the Hostages," *New York Times*, February 22, 1980, 11.

16. Bernard Nossiter, "Trying to Launch Inquiry, UN Copes with Chaos," *New York Times*, February 24, 1980, 137.

17. Bernard Gwertzman, "Deluded or Not, the US Keeps Hoping; Waffling Part Two," *New York Times*, March 2, 1980, E1.

A WRITER'S REFLECTIONS ON THE NUCLEAR AGE

First published in the December 1981 issue of the *Boston Review*. Available at http://bostonreview.net/archives/BR06.6/hazzard.html.

CANTON MORE FAR

First published December 16, 1967, in the *New Yorker*, 42–49.

PAPYROLOGY AT NAPLES

First published August 29, 1983, in the *New Yorker*, 79–83.

1. Edward Gibbon, *The History of the Decline and Fall of the Roman Empire* (Paris: 1840), 55.

2. See reference under "Papyrus" in *Encyclopedia Britannica* (1911), available at http://penelope.uchicago.edu/Thayer/E/Gazetteer/Periods/Roman/Topics/Daily_Life/writing/papyrus/Britannica_1911*.html.

3. Letter, Horace Walpole to Richard West, June 14, 1740, in *Horace Walpole's Correspondence: The Yale Edition*, vol. 13, 222, 224, available at http://images.library.yale.edu/hwcorrespondence/page.asp?vol=13&seq=294&type=b; http://images.library.yale.edu/hwcorrespondence/page.asp?vol=13&seq=296&type=b.

4. Giacomo Leopardi, *Paralipomeni*, Canto Terzo, 41, in "From the Archive," English trans. David Armstrong, *Herculaneum Archaeology* 5, no. 6 (Summer 2006): 6.

5. Norman Douglas, *Siren Land* (West Drayton, UK: Penguin, 1948), 75.

6. Norman Neuerburg, *Herculaneum to Malibu: A Companion to the Visit of the J. Paul Getty Museum Building* (Malibu: J. Paul Getty Museum, 1975).

THE TUSCAN IN EACH OF US

First published in *An Antipodean Connection*, ed. Gaetano Prampolini and Marie Christine Huber (Genève: Editions Slatkine, 1993), 77–82.

1. James Boswell, *The Life of Samuel Johnson, LLD.: Including A Journal of a Tour to the Hebrides*, ed. G. B. Hill, and Rev. L. F. Powell (London: Oxford at the Clarendon Press, 1934), 2:36, 742.

2. W. B. Yeats, "Mehru," from "Supernatural Songs," in Richard J. Finneran, *W. B. Yeats, The Poems*, ed. Richard J. Finneran (London: Macmillan, 1983), 289.

3. Arthur Hugh Clough, "Amours de Voyage," Canto 2, in *Poems of Arthur Hugh Clough*, ed. F. L. Mulhauser (London: Clarendon Press, 1974), 103.

4. E. M. Forster. *A Passage to India* (London: Penguin, 2005), 265–266.

5. Quoted in Walter Pater, "Winckelmann," in *The Renaissance* (New York: Modern Library 1873), 147–194, 148.

6. Jakob Burkhardt, *Reflections on History*, trans. M. D. Hottinger (Indianapolis: Liberty Fund, 1979), 105.

7. Letter, Niccolò Machiavelli to Francesco Vettori, December 10, 1513, in *Machiavelli: The Chief Works and Others*, ed. Allan Gilbert (Durham, NC: Duke University Press, 1989), 2:915.

8. Patrick White, *Riders in the Chariot* (Sydney: Random House, 2011), 522.

9. Ibid., 128.

10. Folgore da San Gimignano, "Di giugnio," in *I Sonetti Dei Mesi* (Siena: Edizioni Cantagalli, 1991), 45. English translation by Richard Aldington, *A Wreath for San Gemignano* (New York: Duell, Sloan and Pearce, Inc. 1945), 23.

11. Giacomo Leopardi, "L'Infinito," in *Canti: Poems*, trans. Jonathan Galassi (Farrar, Straus and Giroux, 2010), 106.

12. Percy Shelley, Note to "Ode to the West Wind," in *Shelley: Poetical Works*, ed. Thomas Hutchinson (London: Oxford University Press, 1970), 577.

2003 NATIONAL BOOK AWARD ACCEPTANCE

National Book Award 2003 Acceptance, available at http://www.nationalbook.org/nbaacceptspeech_shazzard.html#.VLogJ8Yqq9Y. Shirley Hazzard spoke these words on being announced winner of the 2003 National Book Award. She spoke immediately after author Stephen King's speech accepting an award for lifetime achievement.

THE NEW YORK SOCIETY LIBRARY DISCUSSION, SEPTEMBER 2012

On September 7, 2012, as part of the first international symposium on Shirley Hazzard, a distinguished panel discussed her life and work. The panel consisted of Gail Jones, Jay Parini, Martin Stannard, Brigitta Olubas, and Annabel Davis-Goff. It was moderated by Jonathan Galassi and introduced by the Australian Consul-General to New York, Phil Scanlan. A recording of this panel, including Shirley Hazzard's comments, is available at https://www.nysoclib.org/events/shirley-hazzard-literary-icon.

INDEX

824.914 Haz
Hazzard, Shirley, 1931-
We need silence to find out
what we think

Jan 2016